# Communications
# in Computer and Information Science

**2007**

## Rationale

The CCIS series is devoted to the publication of proceedings of computer science conferences. Its aim is to efficiently disseminate original research results in informatics in printed and electronic form. While the focus is on publication of peer-reviewed full papers presenting mature work, inclusion of reviewed short papers reporting on work in progress is welcome, too. Besides globally relevant meetings with internationally representative program committees guaranteeing a strict peer-reviewing and paper selection process, conferences run by societies or of high regional or national relevance are also considered for publication.

## Topics

The topical scope of CCIS spans the entire spectrum of informatics ranging from foundational topics in the theory of computing to information and communications science and technology and a broad variety of interdisciplinary application fields.

## Information for Volume Editors and Authors

Publication in CCIS is free of charge. No royalties are paid, however, we offer registered conference participants temporary free access to the online version of the conference proceedings on SpringerLink (http://link.springer.com) by means of an http referrer from the conference website and/or a number of complimentary printed copies, as specified in the official acceptance email of the event.

CCIS proceedings can be published in time for distribution at conferences or as postproceedings, and delivered in the form of printed books and/or electronically as USBs and/or e-content licenses for accessing proceedings at SpringerLink. Furthermore, CCIS proceedings are included in the CCIS electronic book series hosted in the SpringerLink digital library at http://link.springer.com/bookseries/7899. Conferences publishing in CCIS are allowed to use Online Conference Service (OCS) for managing the whole proceedings lifecycle (from submission and reviewing to preparing for publication) free of charge.

## Publication process

The language of publication is exclusively English. Authors publishing in CCIS have to sign the Springer CCIS copyright transfer form, however, they are free to use their material published in CCIS for substantially changed, more elaborate subsequent publications elsewhere. For the preparation of the camera-ready papers/files, authors have to strictly adhere to the Springer CCIS Authors' Instructions and are strongly encouraged to use the CCIS LaTeX style files or templates.

## Abstracting/Indexing

CCIS is abstracted/indexed in DBLP, Google Scholar, EI-Compendex, Mathematical Reviews, SCImago, Scopus. CCIS volumes are also submitted for the inclusion in ISI Proceedings.

## How to start

To start the evaluation of your proposal for inclusion in the CCIS series, please send an e-mail to ccis@springer.com.

Xiaobing Li · Xiaohong Guan · Yun Tie ·
Xinran Zhang · Qingwen Zhou

Editors

# Music Intelligence

Second Summit, SOMI 2023
Beijing, China, October 28–30, 2023
Revised Selected Papers

*Editors*
Xiaobing Li
Central Conservatory of Music
Beijing, China

Yun Tie
Zhengzhou University
Zhengzhou, China

Qingwen Zhou
Central Conservatory of Music
Beijing, China

Xiaohong Guan
Xi'an Jiaotong University
Xi'an, China

Xinran Zhang ⓘ
Central Conservatory of Music
Beijing, China

ISSN 1865-0929        ISSN 1865-0937 (electronic)
Communications in Computer and Information Science
ISBN 978-981-97-0575-7        ISBN 978-981-97-0576-4 (eBook)
https://doi.org/10.1007/978-981-97-0576-4

This Springer imprint is published by the registered company Springer Nature Singapore Pte Ltd.
The registered company address is: 152 Beach Road, #21-01/04 Gateway East, Singapore 189721, Singapore

Paper in this product is recyclable.

# Preface

Welcome to SOMI 2023, the second Summit on Music Intelligence. SOMI was jointly organized by the Central Conservatory of Music (CCOM) and the Chinese Association for Artificial Intelligence (CAAI). It serves as an important event to bring together leading specialists and researchers from the academic and industrial worlds, share the latest research works, and promote technical innovations. The first SOMI was successfully held in Beijing (2021). Following the previous event, this year's SOMI was again held in Beijing to promote interdisciplinary research between music and artificial intelligence (AI), neural science, and clinical therapy technologies.

SOMI 2023 began with an opening ceremony and concert in CCOM under the caption of "the Music of the Future" with the joint effort of music composers, performance artists, scientists, and engineers, exploring multiple innovative and cutting-edge technologies to promote music composing and performance. Following that, we were honored to have six internationally renowned speakers, Yike Guo (Hong Kong University of Science and Technology), Songchun Zhu (Peking University), Xiaoqin Wang (Tsinghua University), Shihab Shamma (University of Maryland), Maosong Sun (Tsinghua University), and Jiang Li (Huawei), to share their latest achievements and insights in music intelligence. In later events, we organized seven specialized forums, one satellite conference on music therapy, and one roundtable discussion. We also organized the electronic music competition and the electronic music marathon events.

SOMI 2023 (main conference and the satellite conference, science and technology track) received paper submissions under the following topics: novel music AI datasets, models, tasks, and evaluation methods; interdisciplinary research in music and brain science, neuroscience, and psychology; research on artificial intelligence and music healing technologies and clinical applications; big data modeling technology and quantitative analysis technology for music; novel music information retrieval technology; intelligent music composing and producing technology; novel industry applications, industry standards, and prototypes of music artificial intelligence; music artificial intelligence and music perception and music aesthetics. We received 27 valid submissions. Each submission was assigned three different reviewers (double-blinded). After a thorough reviewing process, 10 submissions were accepted, resulting in an acceptance rate of 37.0%. All these submissions were presented as oral papers at the conference. The best paper award was assigned to the submission with the highest overall reviewing score and will be recommended to a special issue of IEEE Transactions on Computational Social Systems. In parallel, we also received 15 submissions in the field of art and social science. They were reviewed on-site in the conference by a different reviewing committee, and 6 submissions were awarded. These submissions were not included in this manuscript.

We thank all reviewers and organizers for their efforts in SOMI 2023. We sincerely thank all 22 reviewers for their valuable time and informative reviews, which guarantee the quality of the proceedings. We are also grateful that the academic committee members, Qionghai Dai (Tsinghua University), Xiaohong Guan (Xi'an Jiaotong University),

Bin Hu (Beijing Institute of Technology), Wei Li (Fudan University), Xiaobing Li (Central Conservatory of Music), Maosong Sun (Tsinghua University), and Songchun Zhu (Peking University) warmly recommended reviewers for our submissions.

We also sincerely thank all the authors who submitted their works to SOMI 2023. Your contributions were all valuable and important for our event. We were really glad to see you in Beijing at SOMI 2023.

November 2023

Xiaobing Li<br>Xinran Zhang

# Organization

## General Chairs

| | |
|---|---|
| Feng Yu | Central Conservatory of Music, China |
| Qionghai Dai | Tsinghua University, China |

## Chief Director

| | |
|---|---|
| Hongmei Yu | Central Conservatory of Music, China |

## Organizing Committee

| | |
|---|---|
| Jianhua Miao | Central Conservatory of Music, China |
| Wenchen Qin | Central Conservatory of Music, China |
| Chunmei Liu | Central Conservatory of Music, China |
| Yang Ke | Central Conservatory of Music, China |

## Executive Chair

| | |
|---|---|
| Xiaobing Li | Central Conservatory of Music, China |

## Academic Committee

| | |
|---|---|
| Qionghai Dai | Tsinghua University, China |
| Xiaohong Guan | Xi'an Jiaotong University, China |
| Bin Hu | Beijing Institute of Technology, China |
| Israel Nelken | Hebrew University of Jerusalem, Israel |
| Wei Li | Fudan University, China |
| Xiaobing Li | Central Conservatory of Music, China |
| Maosong Sun | Tsinghua University, China |
| Shihab Shamma | University of Maryland, USA |
| Xiaoqin Wang | Tsinghua University, China |

| | |
|---|---|
| Xihong Wu | Peking University, China |
| Feng Yu | Central Conservatory of Music, China |
| Songchun Zhu | Peking University, China |

## Directors

| | |
|---|---|
| Xin Wang | Central Conservatory of Music, China |
| Hengjian Fang | Central Conservatory of Music, China |
| Weining Wang | Beijing University of Posts and Telecommunications, China |

## Public Relations Chair

| | |
|---|---|
| Qian Tao | Central Conservatory of Music, China |

## Program Committee Chair

| | |
|---|---|
| Jia Luan | Shandong Normal University, China |

## Publication Chairs

| | |
|---|---|
| Xiaobing Li | Central Conservatory of Music, China |
| Xiaohong Guan | Xi'an Jiaotong University, China |
| Yun Tie | Zhengzhou University, China |
| Xinran Zhang | Central Conservatory of Music, China |
| Qingwen Zhou | Central Conservatory of Music, China |

## Program Committee

| | |
|---|---|
| Jing Chen | Peking University, China |
| Qunxi Dong | Beijing Institute of Technology, China |
| Youtian Du | Xi'an Jiaotong University, China |
| Honglei Guo | Tsinghua University, China |
| Xin Jin | Beijing Electronic Science and Technology Institute, China |
| Wei Li | Fudan University, China |
| Jiafeng Liu | Central Conservatory of Music, China |

| | |
|---|---|
| Kun Qian | Beijing Institute of Technology, China |
| Yun Tie | Zhengzhou University, China |
| Xiaohua Wan | Beijing Institute of Technology, China |
| Chenxu Wang | Xi'an Jiaotong University, China |
| Yuwang Wang | Tsinghua University, China |
| Bing Wei | Central Conservatory of Music, China |
| Xiaoying Zhang | China Rehabilitation Research Center, China |
| Xiaoyu Xia | PLA General Hospital, China |
| Duo Xu | Tianjin Conservatory of Music, China |
| Long Ye | Communication University of China, China |
| Tao Yu | Tsinghua University, China |
| Qin Zhang | Communication University of China, China |
| Xinran Zhang | Central Conservatory of Music, China |
| Ziya Zhou | Hong Kong University of Science and Technology, China |
| Zhong Zhu | Tianjin Huanhu Hospital, China |

## Organizers

## Organized by

Central Conservatory of Music

Chinese Association for Artificial Intelligence

## In Cooperation with

Springer

Communications in Computer and Information Science

# Contents

# Music, Neural Science and Music Therapy

# Musical Training Changes the Intra- and Inter-network Functional Connectivity

Jiancheng Hou[1,2,3] , Chuansheng Chen[4] , and Qi Dong[2(✉)]

[1] Fujian Normal University, Fuzhou Fujian 350007, China
[2] Beijing Normal University, Beijing 100875, China
dongqi@bnu.edu.cn
[3] Indiana University, Bloomington, IN 47405, USA
[4] University of California, Irvine, CA 92697, USA

**Abstract.** Previous studies have evidenced that musical training can change the brain functional and structural organizations, but it is still unclear how interactions within and between functional networks are affected by musical training. Using the resting-state fMRI dataset with a relatively large sample, the present study examined the effects of musical training on inter- and intra-network functional connectivity (FC). The results revealed the decreased inter- and intra-network FC extensively which reflect greater movement efficiency and automaticity as well as five pairs of increased inter-network FC that possibly refer to cognitive function in participants with musical training compared to their counterparts without musical training. The current study provided a new perspective that musical training can induce the brain network changes.

**Keywords:** Musical Training · Resting-State fMRI · Brain Network

## 1 Introduction

Musical training has been greatly evidenced its benefits to cognitive ability (e.g., language, mathematics, reasoning, time perception, executive functions) [1–4] and emotion perception [5, 6]. With the approaches such as electroencephalogram, magnetoencephalography, neuroimaging and near-infrared spectroscopy, lots of neuroscience literature have proved the positive effects of musical training on brain functions and structures that link to these abilities [7–9].

Many studies employed the resting-state functional magnetic resonance imaging (RS-fMRI) to examine the effect of musical training on neural functions. RS-fMRI mainly measures the low-frequency spontaneous during brain neural activity [10], and it can reflect the neural function [11–13]. Some studies have examined the discrepancy of RS-functional connectivity (RSFC) between musicians and non-musicians or the RSFC plasticity by musical training; Luo et al. (2012) used the region of interest (ROI)-analysis method and found the increased RSFC in the motor, auditory, visual and somatosensory network, respectively, in musicians compared to non-musicians. Hou et al. (2015) used the ROI-based method and found the increased RSFC with the seed regions-related to pitch identification ability (e.g., the right dorsolateral prefrontal cortex, bilateral premotor areas, bilateral intraparietal sulcus) in the individuals with musical training, which indicate their specific cognitive strategies such as phonology, auditory coding, vision, semantics and executive functions involved in pitch identification, compared to the individuals without musical training.

However, the seed-based RSFC only provides information about functional interactions between specific brain regions; its analysis usually requires a priori ROI definition and the results strongly depend upon or are limited by ROI chosen [14, 15]. Moreover, the human brain constitutes a whole network and a local organization (e.g., short-range connections) is integrated with the large architecture (e.g., long-range connections) in order to support the high-level cognitive functions in brain [16, 17]. As far as we known, relatively less RS-fMRI studies have investigated the effect of musical training on human network; Luo et al. (2014) found the increased local RSFC density between the regions (e.g., the bilateral anterior insula, dorsal anterior cingulate cortex, anterior temporoparietal junction) which belong to the salience network and are associated with attentional processing and cognitive control, in fifteen profession musicians compared to non-musicians; Li et al. (2018) showed the increased RSFC within the sensorimotor and the auditory-motor networks in twenty-nine novice young adults who accepted 24-week piano training when compared to twenty-seven young adults without training, and the RSFC changes in the sensorimotor network was positively correlated with the piano practice time.

Network science, which is fast-growing, mainly investigates the elements and their interactions or relationships and it has been employed to study the human brain as one kind of complex system. The present study aimed to examine the RS-fMRI whole-brain network FC discrepancy between the individuals with and without musical training. Moreover, the sample size in current study was relatively large, because the small sample size generally lacks the statistical power to detect false positives or small effects so can lead to result diversities [18, 19].

## 2  Methods

### 2.1  Participants

Three hundred and twenty undergraduate students (129 males and 191 females, mean age 20.45 ± SD 1.18 years, age range: 19 ~ 24 years) accepted the RS-fMRI scan. Among them, fifty-six participants had musical training experience (e.g., keyword, violin, piano, accordion, etc.) and their mean starting training age was 10.67 ± 1.44 years (8–20 years). Two hundred and sixty-four participants were without musical training experience. All participants were right-handed measured by the Handedness Inventory [20]. All participants were normal or corrected-to-normal vision and without psychiatric or neurological disease. All participants provided their informed written consent before scanning. Table 1 shows participants' basic demographic information. This study was approved by the Institutional Review Board of the State Key Lab of Cognitive Neuroscience and Learning at Beijing Normal University.

**Table 1.** Participants' basic demographic information.

| Characteristics | Mean (SD) | | $t_{(318)}$ | $p$ |
|---|---|---|---|---|
| | Training | No Training | | |
| Age (years) | 20.68 (1.70) | 20.25 (1.96) | 0.74 | .41 |
| Gender (male/female) | 56 (11/45) | 264 (118/146) | | |
| Handedness | All right-handed | | | |
| Head motion (mean FD_Power) | 0.13 (0.06) | 0.11 (0.05) | 1.44 | .15 |

Note: Standard deviations are shown in parentheses

## 2.2 MRI Data Collection

Data were collected through a 3T Siemens MRI scanner at Beijing Normal University. The parameters of RS-fMRI were: repetition time (TR) = 2000 ms, echo time (TE) = 25 ms, $\theta = 90°$, field of view (FOV) = 192 × 192 mm, matrix = 64 × 64, slice thickness = 3 mm. The parameters of collected anatomical T1-weighted MRI data were: TR = 2530 ms, TE = 3.09 ms, $\theta = 10°$, FOV = 256 × 256 mm, matrix = 256 × 256, slice thickness = 1 mm, sagittal slices = 208. All participants were awake, but only one participant slept (so this scan data was not used), during the scan.

## 2.3 Data Preprocessing

The toolbox of Data Processing and Analysis of Brain Imaging (DPABI, V6.0, http://rfmri.org/dpabi), which also includes a sub-toolbox of Data Processing Assistant for Resting-state fMRI (DPARSF, Advanced Version 5.3), was used for RS-fMRI data preprocessing [21, 22]. DPARSF is a plug-in software that works with Statistical Parametric Mapping (SPM, V12, https://www.fil.ion.ucl.ac.uk/spm/software/spm12/) and Matlab [23]. The first five volumes from the original data were discarded to allow the magnetization to approach a dynamic equilibrium, so the participants could accustom to the scanner noise. Then the parameters (e.g., TR, slice number, voxel size et al.) were set. The preprocessing steps included slice timing, realignment, regressing out head motion parameters (scrubbing with Friston 24-parameter model regression; bad time points were identified using a threshold of frame-wise displacement >0.2 mm, and 1 volume before and 2 volumes after at the individual-subject level as well as accounting for head motion at the group-level (covariate analysis)) [22, 24, 25] and spatial normalization (to the MNI template, resampling voxel size of 3 × 3 × 3 mm) [23, 26]. The temporal correlations as spontaneous connectivity was calculated to quantify RSFC. The symmetric correlation matrixes was calculated through the Dosenbach atlas, which defines 142 regions or nodes across the brain, so a 142 × 142 network matrix was generated per participant [27]. Based on the matrix, each participant had a total of 20,164 unique pairwise functional connectivity, but only half of the pairwise RSFC was used for further analysis because the bottom left half and top right half were the same.

### 2.4 Network Functional Connectivity Construction

We then constructed each participant's network functional connectivity (FC) with the DPABINet V1.1 that is integrated in DPABI V6.0. The 142 nodes in the Dosenbach atlas were classified into seven subnetworks: visual network (VN), somatosensory network (SMN), dorsal attention network (DAN), ventral attention network (VAN), default mode network (DMN), subcortical network (SC), and frontoparietal network (FPN) [28]. Based on the $142 \times 142$ matrix produced at the preprocessing step, the network FC for any pair of two nodes was calculated through the Pearson's linear correlation coefficient, then the Fisher-$z$ transformation was used for the symmetric correlation matrix.

### 2.5 Statistical Analysis

The network FC difference between two groups performed in DPABINet. The statistical analysis was performed by multiple comparison correction and permutation false discovery rate (FDR) $p < .05$ in DPABINet. The results were visualized by DPABINet Viewer. Head motion (mean framewise displacement [FD] values) and gender were considered as covariates.

## 3 Results

### 3.1 Intra-network Functional Connectivity

Table 1 and Figs. 1, 2 and 3 show the significant intra-network FC differences between the two groups. Compared to the participants without musical training, the participants with musical training had significantly decreased intra-network FC between the right dorsal frontal cortex and right supplementary motor area, between the right temporal cortex and left temporal, all of which are within the SMN; the right ventral frontal cortex and left basal ganglia, left middle frontal cortex, right pre-supplementary motor area, respectively, all of which are within the VAN; the left ventral frontal cortex and left occipital cortex that are within the DAN; the left ventromedial prefrontal cortex and left anterior prefrontal cortex as well as the left posterior cingulate cortex that are within the DMN.

**Table 2.** The significant group differences of network FC between participants with vs. no musical training

| Nodes | | Networks | | $t$ value | $p$ *value* |
|---|---|---|---|---|---|
| R dorsal frontal cortex | L ventral frontal cortex | FPN | DAN | 3.4877 | 0.0006 |
| R dorsal frontal cortex | L parietal lobule | FPN | DAN | 3.7306 | 0.0006 |
| R frontal cortex | L precentral cortex | VAN | SMN | 3.4592 | 0.0008 |
| L dorsal frontal cortex | R supplementary motor area | FPN | SMN | 4.0677 | 0.0002 |
| L basal ganglia | L intraparietal sulcus | SC | DMN | 3.7270 | 0.0002 |
| R dorsal frontal cortex | R supplementary motor area | SMN | SMN | −4.2089 | 0.0002 |
| R temporal cortex | L temporal cortex | SMN | SMN | −3.6259 | 0.0004 |
| R temporal cortex | L temporal cortex | SMN | SMN | −3.9575 | 0.0004 |
| R ventral frontal cortex | L basal ganglia | VAN | VAN | −3.3418 | 0.0006 |
| R ventral frontal cortex | L middle frontal cortex | VAN | VAN | −3.6819 | 0.0002 |
| R ventral frontal cortex | R pre-supplementary motor area | VAN | VAN | −3.9249 | 0.0002 |
| L ventral frontal cortex | L occipital cortex | DAN | DAN | −4.3150 | 0.0002 |
| L ventromedial prefrontal cortex | L anterior prefrontal cortex | DMN | DMN | −3.4742 | 0.0004 |
| L posterior cingulate cortex | L posterior cingulate cortex | DMN | DMN | −3.7622 | 0.0004 |
| R dorsal frontal cortex | L basal ganglia | SMN | VAN | −3.6163 | 0.0008 |
| R dorsal frontal cortex | L middle frontal cortex | SMN | VAN | −3.6178 | 0.0004 |
| R dorsal frontal cortex | L anterior insula | SMN | VAN | −3.5387 | 0.0006 |
| R dorsal frontal cortex | R ventral frontal cortex | SMN | VAN | −3.6416 | 0.0002 |
| R supplementary motor area | R ventral frontal cortex | SMN | VAN | −3.4498 | 0.0006 |
| L temporal cortex | R ventral frontal cortex | SMN | VAN | −4.8633 | 0.0002 |

*(continued)*

**Table 2.** (*continued*)

| Nodes | | Networks | | *t* value | *p value* |
|---|---|---|---|---|---|
| R dorsal frontal cortex | L ventral frontal cortex | FPN | DAN | 3.4877 | 0.0006 |
| R dorsal frontal cortex | L precentral cortex | SMN | DAN | −4.3843 | 0.0002 |
| R parietal lobule | L posterior parietal lobule | SMN | DAN | −3.7801 | 0.0002 |
| L parietal lobule | L posterior parietal lobule | SMN | DAN | −3.7665 | 0.0006 |
| R ventral frontal cortex | L precentral cortex | VAN | DAN | −3.6355 | 0.0004 |
| R frontal cortex | R precuneus | VAN | DMN | −3.7133 | 0.0004 |
| L anterior cingulate cortex | L posterior parietal lobule | FPN | DAN | −3.2661 | 0.0004 |
| L ventral anterior prefrontal cortex | R angular gyrus | FPN | DMN | −3.4821 | 0.0008 |
| L ventral frontal cortex | L posterior cingulate cortex | FPN | DMN | −3.8021 | 0.0008 |
| L occipital cortex | R occipital cortex | FPN | VN | −4.6311 | 0.0002 |
| L posterior cingulate cortex | R occipital cortex | DMN | VN | −3.5926 | 0.0006 |
| R precuneus | R occipital cortex | DMN | VN | −3.6283 | 0.0002 |
| R posterior cingulate cortex | R occipital cortex | DMN | VN | −4.4297 | 0.0002 |
| L posterior cingulate cortex | R occipital cortex | DMN | VN | −4.2103 | 0.0004 |
| R occipital cortex | R occipital cortex | DMN | VN | −3.3786 | 0.0004 |
| R precuneus | L posterior parietal lobule | DMN | DAN | −3.7976 | 0.0002 |

Note: VN: visual network; SMN; somatosensory network; VAN: ventral attention network; DAN: dorsal attention network; DMN: default mode network; SC: subcortical network; FPN: frontoparietal network; L: left; R: right

## 3.2 Inter-network Functional Connectivity

Table 2 and Figs. 1, 2 and 3 shows the significant inter-network FC differences between the two groups. Compared to the participants without musical training, the participants with musical training had significantly decreased inter-network FC between the SMN and VAN, SMN and DAN, VAN and DAN, VAN and DMN, FPN and DAN, FPN and DMN, FPN and VN, DMN and VN, DMN and DAN. Moreover, there also had a few significantly increased inter-network FC between the FPN and DAN, VAN and SMN, FPN and SMN, and DMN and SC in the participants with musical training compared to those without training.

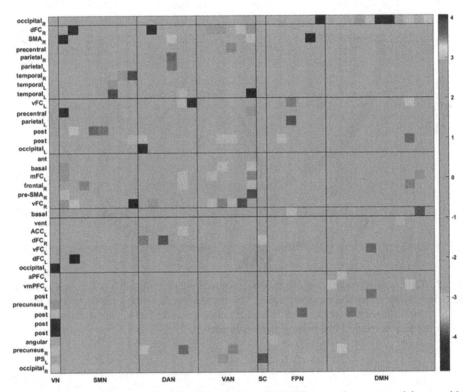

**Fig. 1.** The matrix of network functional connectivity (FC) differences between participants with vs. without musical training. The color bar indicates the FC value. Positive value means training had increased network FC than no training, negative value means training had decreased network FC than no training. VN: visual network; SMN; somatosensory network; VAN: ventral attention network; DAN: dorsal attention network; DMN: default mode network; SC: subcortical network; FPN: frontoparietal network; L: left; R: right.

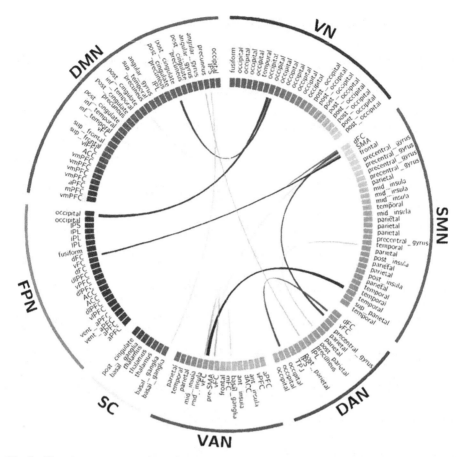

**Fig. 2.** The circus representation of network functional connectivity (FC) differences between participants with vs. without musical training. VN: visual network; SMN; somatosensory network; VAN: ventral attention network; DAN: dorsal attention network; DMN: default mode network; SC: subcortical network; FPN: frontoparietal network.

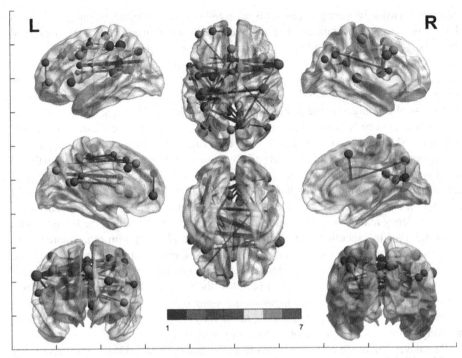

**Fig. 3.** The brain network functional connectivity (FC) differences between participants with vs. without musical training. Red line means training had increased network FC than no training, blue line means training had decreased network FC than no training. VN: visual network; SMN; somatosensory network; VAN: ventral attention network; DAN: dorsal attention network; DMN: default mode network; SC: subcortical network; FPN: frontoparietal network.

## 4   Discussion

Using a relatively large sample size of participants, the present study revealed the decreased intra- and inter-network FC extensively, and only five pairs of increased inter-network FC, in participants with musical training compared to the participants without musical training.

### 4.1   Intra-network Functional Connectivity

The present results were contrary to our original hypothesis that the participants with musical training should have increased intra-network FC than those without training. Many RSFC studies have shown that musicians have increased RSFC between the multiple sensory (e.g., auditory, vision and somatosensory) and motor cortices which indicate the enhanced cognitive integration between the lower-level perception and motor function [29], or have greater RSFC that relates to salience system which is associated with higher-level attention and cognitive control [30], than non-musicians. Moreover, there have the increased RSFC that involves motor control, working memory, vision and auditory in individuals with musical training [31], or have the increased dynamic visual and auditory network in young adults who accepted a 24-week piano training [16], than those without musical training. But relatively less studies have shown the decreased RSFC between musicians and non-musicians; for example, the RSFC between the right frontal cortex seed and the left precentral gyrus, right supplementary motor area, left temporal gyrus and right precuneus, which are associated with emotion, spatial cognition, motor control, sensory processing and visual perception, were observed in participants with musical training than the participants without training (Hou et al. 2015).

The present results showed that the training group had decreased intra-network FC within the SMN, VAN, DAN and DMN that comprise the regions such as basal ganglia, supplementary motor area, precuneus and posterior cingulate cortex, compared to the no training group. Some studies have shown that cognitive training induces the reduction of neural activities that include the basal ganglia [32], supplementary motor area, parietal cortex [33, 34] and posterior cingulate cortex [35], which reflect the improved movement efficiency and automaticity after training [32, 36–38]. In detail, the basal ganglia plays the roles in execution and control of movement [32, 39] with other motor areas (e.g., the supplementary and primary motor cortex, dorsal frontal cortex) [40, 41]; the supplementary motor area is important to learn by imitation, mediate perception/action coupling and control body movement [42, 43]; the posterior cingulate cortex, a center region in DMN which also encompasses the ventromedial prefrontal cortex, anterior prefrontal cortex, angular gyrus, middle temporal gyrus, precuneus etc. [44], refers to working memory, emotion, vision and motor perception [45].

Moreover, the decreased intra-network FC within the SMN, DMN, VAN and DAN in current study are also contrary to other studies about that musical training induces increased SMN [16, 29, 46, 47], DMN [46, 48], VAN and DAN [49]. Many factors could be the latencies to this contrary such as sample size, gender difference, number of connectives or the degree of myelin formation, which can interact with MRI processing and signals [50–52]. In addition, the reduced intra-network FC possibly also reflects the greater efficiency and automaticity benefited from musical training. Indeed, in a structural MRI study, compared to the non-musicians, musicians had the decreased gray matter density (e.g., the inferior temporal gyrus, inferior occipital gyrus, fusiform, perirolandic cortex, stratum, caudate nucleus) [53], which refer to visual and sensorimotor functions and reflect their less non-pertinent visual or sensorimotor feedback in order to improve the efficiency and automaticity relative to musical movement, perception and performance profited from musical training [53–55]. Some studies found the DMN decrease after motor imagery training, illustrating the improved cognitive efficiency with less neural activity [32, 56], or the improved regulating ability to introspective thought after training [57, 58], or the attenuated integration of information from other resting-state networks [59, 60]. The SMN is responsible for motor, somatosensory, visual and auditory processing [61] and its decreased network FC may reflect the enhanced cognitive efficiency along the shortest neural path in brain [32, 62, 63]. The DAN and VAN are engaged during attention involved [64, 65]; a meta-analysis showed that the decrease in attentional network are related to the reduced demands on externally focused attention through motor skill training [64].

## 4.2  Inter-network Functional Connectivity

In present study, the participants with musical training had significantly increased inter-network FC between the FPN and DAN, VAN and SMN, FPN and SMN, DMN and SC than the participants without musical training. Studies have proved that musical training benefits to the cognitive abilities such as executive control, working memory, language and attention (D'Souza et al., 2018; Moreno et al., 2011; Sala & Gobet, 2020; Shen et al., 2019). The inter-network FC between the FPN and SMN [66], and between the FPN and DAN, refer to working memory to facilitate movement control [67]. The inter-network FC between the FPN and DAN is associated with executive function and attention [68] that combines with the dopamine release [69]. Moreover, the inter-network FC between the FPN and DAN, between the SC (be responsible for attention) [70] and DMN, are involved the reward function [71]. Studies have found the role of dopamine in reward [72, 73] and musical training has been evidenced its role in the dopamine release (especially the D4 receptors) [74–76] that benefits to sensory processing and reward cognition [73, 77].

Nevertheless, the participants with musical training had many decreased inter-network FC than the participants without musical training. Wang et al. (2015) divided the networks into higher-level order that includes the DMN and FPN as well as the lower-level order that includes the SMN and VN. Although the reasons to the reduced inter-network (especially between the higher- and lower-network) FC after training remain to be unclear, it may be related to the decoupling of different networks that avoid the interaction with each other under specific cognitive conditions [62, 78, 79], or may be the rapid information integration and improved cognitive efficiency along the shortest neural path between brain networks [63]. In detail, the inter-network FC between FPN and VN reflects the improved effective transformation from visual input to the coordinates for motor behavior [80]; the decreased DMN and VN inter-network reflects the monitoring or balancing the internal introspective thought and external task requirement without more attention or distraction involved [78, 81]; the decreased inter-network FC between the FPN and DMN possibly indicates the maintenance of cognitive control after training but without the disturbance by internal cognition such as introspection or self-awareness [32, 82].

## 4.3  Limitation

The present study also had some limitations. First, only non-musicians were collected, so it is unclear whether the present results can be applied to musicians. Second, the detailed information (e.g., how many years about participants' musical training, whether they continued to practice instruments) was not collected, so future research should deeply examine these relationships with brain network. Third, the RS-fMRI time series was measured by the correlational approach so the causal relationship between the brain networks are unknown. Future work can employ the structural equation modeling or Granger causality to examine the directional FC among networks [32].

## 5  Conclusion

With the resting-state fMRI dataset and a relatively large sample, the current study showed that musical training extensively induces the decreased intra- and inter-network functional connectivity which reflect greater movement efficiency and automaticity as well as a few increased inter-networks functional connectivity that possibly refer to cognitive function when compared to no musical training. The current study provided a new perspective that musical training can reorganize the brain network plasticity.

**Acknowledgments.** This study was supported by the 111 Project from the Ministry of Education of China (B07008). We thank all graduate research assistants who helped us with data collection.

**Disclosure of Interests.** All authors have no conflicting interests.

## References

1. D'Souza, A.A., Moradzadeh, L., Wiseheart, M.: Musical training, bilingualism, and executive function: working memory and inhibitory control. Cogn. Res. Princ. Implic. **3**, 11 (2018). https://doi.org/10.1186/s41235-018-0095-6
2. Shen, Y., Lin, Y., Liu, S., Fang, L., Liu, G.: Sustained effect of music training on the enhancement of executive function in preschool children. Front. Psychol. **10**, 1910 (2019). https://doi.org/10.3389/fpsyg.2019.01910
3. Moreno, S., et al.: Short-term music training enhances verbal intelligence and executive function. Psychol. Sci. **22**, 1425–1433 (2011). https://doi.org/10.1177/0956797611416999
4. Sala, G., Gobet, F.: Cognitive and academic benefits of music training with children: a multilevel meta-analysis. Mem. Cognit. **48**, 1429–1441 (2020). https://doi.org/10.3758/s13421-020-01060-2
5. Di Mauro, M., Toffalini, E., Grassi, M., Petrini, K.: Effect of long-term music training on emotion perception from drumming improvisation. Front. Psychol. **9**, 2168 (2018). https://doi.org/10.3389/fpsyg.2018.02168
6. Schellenberg, E.G., Mankarious, M.: Music training and emotion comprehension in childhood. Emotion **12**, 887–891 (2012). https://doi.org/10.1037/a0027971
7. Rodrigues, A.C., Loureiro, M.A., Caramelli, P.: Musical training, neuroplasticity and cognition. Dement Neuropsychol. **4**, 277–286 (2010). https://doi.org/10.1590/S1980-57642010DN40400005
8. Hyde, K.L., et al.: The effects of musical training on structural brain development: a longitudinal study. Ann. N. Y. Acad. Sci. **1169**, 182–186 (2009). https://doi.org/10.1111/j.1749-6632.2009.04852.x
9. Choi, U.S., Sung, Y.W., Ogawa, S.: Brain plasticity reflects specialized cognitive development induced by musical training. Cereb Cortex Commun. **2**, tgab037 (2021). https://doi.org/10.1093/texcom/tgab037
10. Lv, Y.T., et al.: Correlations in spontaneous activity and gray matter density between left and right sensoritmotor areas of pianists. NeuroReport **19**, 631–634 (2008). https://doi.org/10.1097/WNR.0b013e3282fa6da0
11. Damoiseaux, J.S., et al.: Consistent resting-state networks across healthy subjects. Proc Natl Acad Sci U S A. **103**, 13848–13853 (2006). https://doi.org/10.1073/pnas.0601417103

12. Fox, M.D., Raichle, M.E.: Spontaneous fluctuations in brain activity observed with functional magnetic resonance imaging. Nat. Rev. Neurosci. **8**, 700–711 (2007). https://doi.org/10.1038/nrn2201
13. Zhang, S., Li, C.S.: Functional clustering of the human inferior parietal lobule by whole-brain connectivity mapping of resting-state functional magnetic resonance imaging signals. Brain Connect. **4**, 53–69 (2014). https://doi.org/10.1089/brain.2013.0191
14. Smith, S.M., et al.: Network modelling methods for FMRI. Neuroimage **54**, 875–891 (2011). https://doi.org/10.1016/j.neuroimage.2010.08.063
15. Tian, L., Ren, J., Zang, Y.: Regional homogeneity of resting state fMRI signals predicts Stop signal task performance. Neuroimage **60**, 539–544 (2012). https://doi.org/10.1016/j.neuroimage.2011.11.098
16. Li, Q., et al.: Musical training induces functional and structural auditory-motor network plasticity in young adults. Hum. Brain Mapp. **39**, 2098–2110 (2018). https://doi.org/10.1002/hbm.23989
17. Park, H.J., Friston, K.: Structural and functional brain networks: from connections to cognition. Science **342**, 1238411 (2013). https://doi.org/10.1126/science.1238411
18. Leipold, S., Klein, C., Jancke, L.: Musical expertise shapes functional and structural brain networks independent of absolute pitch ability. J. Neurosci. **41**, 2496–2511 (2021). https://doi.org/10.1523/JNEUROSCI.1985-20.2020
19. Button, K.S., et al.: Power failure: why small sample size undermines the reliability of neuroscience. Nat. Rev. Neurosci. **14**, 365–376 (2013). https://doi.org/10.1038/nrn3475
20. Snyder, P.J., Harris, L.J.: Handedness, sex, and familial sinistrality effects on spatial tasks. Cortex **29**, 115–134 (1993). https://doi.org/10.1016/s0010-9452(13)80216-x
21. Chang, C., Glover, G.H.: Time-frequency dynamics of resting-state brain connectivity measured with fMRI. Neuroimage **50**, 81–98 (2010). https://doi.org/10.1016/j.neuroimage.2009.12.011
22. Yan, C.G., Wang, X.D., Zuo, X.N., Zang, Y.F.: DPABI: data processing & analysis for (resting-state) brain imaging. Neuroinformatics **14**, 339–351 (2016). https://doi.org/10.1007/s12021-016-9299-4
23. Chao-Gan, Y., Yu-Feng, Z.: DPARSF: a MATLAB toolbox for "pipeline" data analysis of resting-state fMRI. Front. Syst. Neurosci. **4**, 13 (2010). https://doi.org/10.3389/fnsys.2010.00013
24. Power, J.D., Barnes, K.A., Snyder, A.Z., Schlaggar, B.L., Petersen, S.E.: Spurious but systematic correlations in functional connectivity MRI networks arise from subject motion. Neuroimage **59**, 2142–2154 (2012). https://doi.org/10.1016/j.neuroimage.2011.10.018
25. Yan, C.G., Craddock, R.C., He, Y., Milham, M.P.: Addressing head motion dependencies for small-world topologies in functional connectomics. Front. Hum. Neurosci. **7**, 910 (2013). https://doi.org/10.3389/fnhum.2013.00910
26. Kuhn, S., Vanderhasselt, M.A., De Raedt, R., Gallinat, J.: Why ruminators won't stop: the structural and resting state correlates of rumination and its relation to depression. J. Affect. Disord. **141**, 352–360 (2012). https://doi.org/10.1016/j.jad.2012.03.024
27. Dosenbach, N.U., et al.: Prediction of individual brain maturity using fMRI. Science **329**, 1358–1361 (2010). https://doi.org/10.1126/science.1194144
28. Yeo, B.T., et al.: The organization of the human cerebral cortex estimated by intrinsic functional connectivity. J. Neurophysiol. **106**, 1125–1165 (2011). https://doi.org/10.1152/jn.00338.2011
29. Luo, C., et al.: Musical training induces functional plasticity in perceptual and motor networks: insights from resting-state FMRI. PLoS ONE **7**, e36568 (2012). https://doi.org/10.1371/journal.pone.0036568
30. Luo, C., et al.: Long-term effects of musical training and functional plasticity in salience system. Neural Plast. **2014**, 180138 (2014). https://doi.org/10.1155/2014/180138

31. Hou, J., Chen, C., Dong, Q.: Resting-state functional connectivity and pitch identification ability in non-musicians. Front. Neurosci. **9**, 7 (2015). https://doi.org/10.3389/fnins.2015.00007

32. Huang, H., et al.: Long-term intensive gymnastic training induced changes in intra- and inter-network functional connectivity: an independent component analysis. Brain Struct. Funct. **223**(1), 131–144 (2017). https://doi.org/10.1007/s00429-017-1479-y

33. Dayan, E., Cohen, L.G.: Neuroplasticity subserving motor skill learning. Neuron **72**, 443–454 (2011). https://doi.org/10.1016/j.neuron.2011.10.008

34. Hardwick, R.M., Rottschy, C., Miall, R.C., Eickhoff, S.B.: A quantitative meta-analysis and review of motor learning in the human brain. Neuroimage **67**, 283–297 (2013). https://doi.org/10.1016/j.neuroimage.2012.11.020

35. Gates, N. J. et al.: Computerised cognitive training for 12 or more weeks for maintaining cognitive function in cognitively healthy people in late life. Cochrane Database Syst Rev. **2**, CD012277 (2020). https://doi.org/10.1002/14651858.CD012277.pub3

36. Hikosaka, O., Nakamura, K., Sakai, K., Nakahara, H.: Central mechanisms of motor skill learning. Curr. Opin. Neurobiol. **12**, 217–222 (2002). https://doi.org/10.1016/s0959-4388(02)00307-0

37. Braunlich, K., Seger, C.: The basal ganglia. Wiley Interdiscip. Rev. Cogn. Sci. **4**, 135–148 (2013). https://doi.org/10.1002/wcs.1217

38. Walz, A.D., et al.: Changes in cortical, cerebellar and basal ganglia representation after comprehensive long term unilateral hand motor training. Behav. Brain Res. **278**, 393–403 (2015). https://doi.org/10.1016/j.bbr.2014.08.044

39. Alexander, G.E., Crutcher, M.D.: Functional architecture of basal ganglia circuits: neural substrates of parallel processing. Trends Neurosci. **13**, 266–271 (1990). https://doi.org/10.1016/0166-2236(90)90107-l

40. Middleton, F.A., Strick, P.L.: Basal-ganglia 'projections' to the prefrontal cortex of the primate. Cereb. Cortex **12**, 926–935 (2002). https://doi.org/10.1093/cercor/12.9.926

41. Leisman, G., Melillo, R.: The basal ganglia: motor and cognitive relationships in a clinical neurobehavioral context. Rev. Neurosci. **24**, 9–25 (2013). https://doi.org/10.1515/revneuro-2012-0067

42. Hou, J., et al.: Mirror neuron activation of musicians and non-musicians in response to motion captured piano performances. Brain Cogn. **115**, 47–55 (2017). https://doi.org/10.1016/j.bandc.2017.04.001

43. Kristeva, R., Chakarov, V., Schulte-Monting, J., Spreer, J.: Activation of cortical areas in music execution and imagining: a high-resolution EEG study. Neuroimage **20**, 1872–1883 (2003). https://doi.org/10.1016/s1053-8119(03)00422-1

44. Peyron, R., Quesada, C., Fauchon, C.: Cingulate-mediated approaches to treating chronic pain. Handb. Clin. Neurol. **166**, 317–326 (2019). https://doi.org/10.1016/B978-0-444-64196-0.00017-0

45. Leech, R., Sharp, D.J.: The role of the posterior cingulate cortex in cognition and disease. Brain. **137**, 12–32 (2014). https://doi.org/10.1093/brain/awt162

46. Alluri, V., et al.: Connectivity patterns during music listening: evidence for action-based processing in musicians. Hum. Brain Mapp. **38**, 2955–2970 (2017). https://doi.org/10.1002/hbm.23565

47. Olszewska, A.M., Gaca, M., Herman, A.M., Jednorog, K., Marchewka, A.: How musical training shapes the adult brain: predispositions and neuroplasticity. Front. Neurosci. **15**, 630829 (2021). https://doi.org/10.3389/fnins.2021.630829

48. Belden, A., et al.: Improvising at rest: Differentiating jazz and classical music training with resting state functional connectivity. Neuroimage **207**, 116384 (2020). https://doi.org/10.1016/j.neuroimage.2019.116384

49. Faller, J., Goldman, A., Lin, Y., McIntosh, J.R., Sajda, P.: Spatiospectral brain networks reflective of improvisational experience. Neuroimage **242**, 118458 (2021). https://doi.org/10.1016/j.neuroimage.2021.118458

50. Bermudez, P., Lerch, J.P., Evans, A.C., Zatorre, R.J.: Neuroanatomical correlates of musicianship as revealed by cortical thickness and voxel-based morphometry. Cereb. Cortex **19**, 1583–1596 (2009). https://doi.org/10.1093/cercor/bhn196

51. Eickhoff, S., et al.: High-resolution MRI reflects myeloarchitecture and cytoarchitecture of human cerebral cortex. Hum. Brain Mapp. **24**, 206–215 (2005). https://doi.org/10.1002/hbm.20082

52. Gittins, R., Harrison, P.J.: A quantitative morphometric study of the human anterior cingulate cortex. Brain Res. **1013**, 212–222 (2004). https://doi.org/10.1016/j.brainres.2004.03.064

53. James, C.E., et al.: Musical training intensity yields opposite effects on grey matter density in cognitive versus sensorimotor networks. Brain Struct. Funct. **219**, 353–366 (2014). https://doi.org/10.1007/s00429-013-0504-z

54. Koutstaal, W., et al.: Perceptual specificity in visual object priming: functional magnetic resonance imaging evidence for a laterality difference in fusiform cortex. Neuropsychologia **39**, 184–199 (2001). https://doi.org/10.1016/s0028-3932(00)00087-7

55. Gaser, C., Schlaug, G.: Brain structures differ between musicians and non-musicians. J. Neurosci. **23**, 9240–9245 (2003)

56. Babiloni, C., et al.: Neural efficiency" of experts' brain during judgment of actions: a high-resolution EEG study in elite and amateur karate athletes. Behav. Brain Res. **207**, 466–475 (2010). https://doi.org/10.1016/j.bbr.2009.10.034

57. Mason, M.F., et al.: Wandering minds: the default network and stimulus-independent thought. Science **315**, 393–395 (2007). https://doi.org/10.1126/science.1131295

58. Taylor, V.A., et al.: Impact of meditation training on the default mode network during a restful state. Soc Cogn Affect Neurosci. **8**, 4–14 (2013). https://doi.org/10.1093/scan/nsr087

59. de Pasquale, F., et al.: The connectivity of functional cores reveals different degrees of segregation and integration in the brain at rest. Neuroimage **69**, 51–61 (2013). https://doi.org/10.1016/j.neuroimage.2012.11.051

60. Li, R., et al.: Large-scale directional connections among multi resting-state neural networks in human brain: a functional MRI and Bayesian network modeling study. Neuroimage **56**, 1035–1042 (2011). https://doi.org/10.1016/j.neuroimage.2011.03.010

61. Li, L., et al.: Eight-week antidepressant treatment reduces functional connectivity in first-episode drug-naive patients with major depressive disorder. Hum. Brain Mapp. **42**, 2593–2605 (2021). https://doi.org/10.1002/hbm.25391

62. Deco, G., Jirsa, V., McIntosh, A.R., Sporns, O., Kotter, R.: Key role of coupling, delay, and noise in resting brain fluctuations. Proc Natl Acad Sci U S A. **106**, 10302–10307 (2009). https://doi.org/10.1073/pnas.0901831106

63. Chen, G., Chen, G., Xie, C., Li, S.J.: Negative functional connectivity and its dependence on the shortest path length of positive network in the resting-state human brain. Brain Connect. **1**, 195–206 (2011). https://doi.org/10.1089/brain.2011.0025

64. Patel, R., Spreng, R.N., Turner, G.R.: Functional brain changes following cognitive and motor skills training: a quantitative meta-analysis. Neurorehabil. Neural Repair **27**, 187–199 (2013). https://doi.org/10.1177/1545968312461718

65. Jolles, D.D., Grol, M.J., Van Buchem, M.A., Rombouts, S.A., Crone, E.A.: Practice effects in the brain: Changes in cerebral activation after working memory practice depend on task demands. Neuroimage **52**, 658–668 (2010). https://doi.org/10.1016/j.neuroimage.2010.04.028

66. Lebedev, A.V., Nilsson, J., Lovden, M.: Working memory and reasoning benefit from different modes of large-scale brain dynamics in healthy older adults. J. Cogn. Neurosci. **30**, 1033–1046 (2018). https://doi.org/10.1162/jocn_a_01260

67. Spreng, R.N., Turner, G.R.: The Shifting Architecture of Cognition and Brain Function in Older Adulthood. Perspect. Psychol. Sci. **14**, 523–542 (2019). https://doi.org/10.1177/174 5691619827511

68. Baggio, H.C., et al.: Cognitive impairment and resting-state network connectivity in Parkinson's disease. Hum. Brain Mapp. **36**, 199–212 (2015). https://doi.org/10.1002/hbm. 22622

69. Trujillo, P., et al.: Dopamine effects on frontal cortical blood flow and motor inhibition in Parkinson's disease. Cortex **115**, 99–111 (2019). https://doi.org/10.1016/j.cortex.2019.01.016

70. Li, L., et al.: Brain functional changes in patients with Crohn's disease: a resting-state fMRI study. Brain Behav. **11**, e2243 (2021). https://doi.org/10.1002/brb3.2243

71. Castellanos, F.X., Aoki, Y.: Intrinsic functional connectivity in attention-deficit/hyperactivity disorder: a science in development. Biol. Psychiatry Cogn. Neurosci. Neuroimaging. **1**, 253–261 (2016). https://doi.org/10.1016/j.bpsc.2016.03.004

72. Baik, J.H.: Stress and the dopaminergic reward system. Exp. Mol. Med. **52**, 1879–1890 (2020). https://doi.org/10.1038/s12276-020-00532-4

73. Ferreri, L., et al.: Dopamine modulates the reward experiences elicited by music. Proc Natl Acad Sci U S A. **116**, 3793–3798 (2019). https://doi.org/10.1073/pnas.1811878116

74. Cocker, P.J., Le Foll, B., Rogers, R.D., Winstanley, C.A.: A selective role for dopamine D(4) receptors in modulating reward expectancy in a rodent slot machine task. Biol. Psychiatry **75**, 817–824 (2014). https://doi.org/10.1016/j.biopsych.2013.08.026

75. Miendlarzewska, E.A., Trost, W.J.: How musical training affects cognitive development: rhythm, reward and other modulating variables. Front Neurosci. **7**, 279 (2013). https://doi. org/10.3389/fnins.2013.00279

76. Nemirovsky, S.I., Avale, M.E., Brunner, D., Rubinstein, M.: Reward-seeking and discrimination deficits displayed by hypodopaminergic mice are prevented in mice lacking dopamine D4 receptors. Synapse. **63**, 991–997 (2009). https://doi.org/10.1002/syn.20680

77. Steele, C.J., Bailey, J.A., Zatorre, R.J., Penhune, V.B.: Early musical training and white-matter plasticity in the corpus callosum: evidence for a sensitive period. J. Neurosci. **33**, 1282–1290 (2013). https://doi.org/10.1523/JNEUROSCI.3578-12.2013

78. Wang, L., Liu, Q., Shen, H., Li, H., Hu, D.: Large-scale functional brain network changes in taxi drivers: evidence from resting-state fMRI. Hum. Brain Mapp. **36**, 862–871 (2015). https://doi.org/10.1002/hbm.22670

79. Lewis, C.M., Baldassarre, A., Committeri, G., Romani, G.L., Corbetta, M.: Learning sculpts the spontaneous activity of the resting human brain. Proc Natl Acad Sci U S A. **106**, 17558–17563 (2009). https://doi.org/10.1073/pnas.0902455106

80. Rizzolatti, G., Matelli, M.: Two different streams form the dorsal visual system: anatomy and functions. Exp. Brain Res. **153**, 146–157 (2003). https://doi.org/10.1007/s00221-003-1588-0

81. Gusnard, D.A., Raichle, M.E., Raichle, M.E.: Searching for a baseline: functional imaging and the resting human brain. Nat. Rev. Neurosci. **2**, 685–694 (2001). https://doi.org/10.1038/ 35094500

82. Leech, R., Kamourieh, S., Beckmann, C.F., Sharp, D.J.: Fractionating the default mode network: distinct contributions of the ventral and dorsal posterior cingulate cortex to cognitive control. J. Neurosci. **31**, 3217–3224 (2011). https://doi.org/10.1523/JNEUROSCI.5626-10. 2011

# Research on the Improvement of Children's Attention Through Binaural Beats Music Therapy in the Context of AI Music Generation

Weijia Yang[1,2] , Chih-Fang Huang[3](✉) , Hsun-Yi Huang[3] ,
Zixue Zhang[4] , Wenjun Li[5] , and Chunmei Wang[1]

[1] Shandong Xiehe University, JINAN 250109, China
[2] Kyonggi University, Seoul 03746, South Korea
[3] Kainan University, Taoyuan City 33857, Taiwan, China
jeffh.me83g@gmail.com
[4] University Putra Malaysia, SELANGOR 43400, Malaysia
[5] Chonnam National University, GWANGJU 61186, South Korea

**Abstract.** In this study, we explored the potential of Binaural Beats Music Therapy (BBMT) augmented with AI-generated music to enhance attention in children diagnosed with Attention Deficit Disorder (ADD). Utilizing a $2 \times 2$ mixed experimental design, we differentiated between traditional and AI-generated music (between-subjects) and incorporated vs. excluded BBMT (within-subjects). We engaged 60 children, averaging 8 years of age, and diagnosed via the SNAP-IV scale. These children were randomly assigned to either the Original Music or AI Music groups, each consisting of 30 participants. Over a 4-week period, with 30-min sessions conducted five days a week, we gauged Heart Rate Variability (HRV) data before and after subjecting each group to their allocated music sessions, integrating BBMT where necessary. Subsequent analysis revealed a marked increase in attention post-intervention. Both music methodologies, when amalgamated with BBMT, significantly bolstered attention levels ($P < 0.05$). Intriguingly, AI music's efficacy paralleled that of its traditional counterpart, underscoring the maturity of AI in music generation and its viability for routine therapeutic application.

**Keywords:** Binaural Beats · Music Therapy · AI Music · Attention Deficit Disorder · Heart Rate Variability

## 1 Introduction

Attention Deficit Disorder (ADD) is a neurodevelopmental disorder, most often diagnosed before the age of seven [6]. Typically, medication is used to help control

Supported by the Ministry of Science and Technology project of Taiwan, China: MOST 111-2320-B-424-002.

the symptoms of this condition. In addition to pharmacological treatments, non-drug therapies like behavioral therapy and music therapy are common treatment modalities. In recent years, numerous scholars have demonstrated the positive impact of music on attention [14]. Existing research has highlighted the particular efficacy of Binaural Beats Music (BB-Music) in enhancing attention [11]. However, most of these studies focus on traditional music, neglecting an exploration of music content [15]. In today's era of artificial intelligence, AI-generated music is at the forefront of content creation and has quickly been adopted in sectors like education, law, and healthcare [16]. Thus, this study integrates "AI music" with "Binaural Beats" to investigate the effects of BBMT under the backdrop of AI music generation on children's attention enhancement. It also offers valuable insights for fields like music education and music therapy. The research primarily addresses the following questions (RQ):

- **RQ1:** Can listening to music enhance children's attention?
- **RQ2:** Does AI-generated music also boost children's attention? How does it differ from conventional music?
- **RQ3:** How effective is BBMT in elevating children's attention?
- **RQ4:** Can AI music also be integrated with BBMT? Is it more effective in improving children's attention?

## 2   Literature Review

### 2.1   ADD and HRV

Attention Deficit Disorder (ADD) is a neurodevelopmental condition, with most cases manifesting before the age of seven. Its primary causes include the late development of the frontal lobe, leading to structural and functional connectivity anomalies, along with abnormalities in neurotransmitter levels, particularly reduced levels of dopamine and norepinephrine. The disorder predominantly manifests as distractibility and forgetfulness [6]. The symptoms of attention deficit can adversely affect a student's academic performance and social behavior. These symptoms can persist into adulthood, potentially impacting one's career and interpersonal relationships, emphasizing the importance of early diagnosis and treatment. ADD is a subtype of Attention Deficit Hyperactivity Disorder (ADHD), characterized mainly by attention deficit without accompanying hyperactivity or impulsiveness. Diagnosis can be conducted using the SNAP-IV assessment scale [1].

Heart Rate Variability (HRV) serves as a measure of the Autonomic Nervous System (ANS) activity. The balance and flexibility of the autonomic nervous system are crucial for physical health and well-being, as detailed by Rajendra Acharya in his 2006 article [17]. An array of factors, ranging from stress, emotional fluxes, sleep cycles, dietary patterns, to physical exertion, can recalibrate the operations of the ANS. A heightened HRV typically resonates with robust health, whereas a diminished HRV can presage ailments such as cardiovascular disorders, autonomic imbalances, and mental stress paradigms. By monitoring

HRV, preemptive insights into health aberrations can be gleaned, facilitating modifications in daily regimens, nutrition, and physical activities to fortify holistic health.

Several studies have observed a link between heart rate variability and symptoms of attention deficit. Ingrid Tonhajzerova et al. (2016) examined the association between attention deficit symptoms and event-related potentials in Electroencephalograms (EEGs), suggesting that ANS dysregulation could be a potential mechanism for these symptoms [20]. Andreea Robe et al. (2019) in their systematic review and meta-analysis found a significant relationship between attention deficit symptoms and ANS dysregulation, especially concerning HRV [19]. The nexus between attention deficits and HRV is distinctly manifest in metrics such as SDNN, rmSSD, pNN50, and LF/HF. It's evident that HRV measurements offer a granular perspective on attention enhancement nuances in ADD.

## 2.2 BBMT Theory

Binaural Beats Music Therapy (BBMT) is a non-invasive therapeutic method relying on auditory stimulation. It operates on the principle where the brain perceives a third frequency when subjected to two different standard frequencies. The key distinction between post Binaural Beats (BB) processed music and conventional music lies in the difference in standard frequencies presented to the left and right brain. The therapy regulates brain activity through music, thereby modulating neurotransmission [5]. BB-Music typically comprises two distinct frequency sine waves delivered separately to each ear, which are transmitted to the auditory cortex via brainstem neurons. Subsequently, the brain synthesizes these two sine waves, resulting in a novel stimulus, termed BB [12]. The frequency of BB usually ranges between 1–30 Hertz (Hz), with input frequencies required to be within 20–1500 Hz. Additionally, both frequencies must be fairly close (with a difference under 30 Hz) to perceive the pulsating beat.

Such auditory stimuli, like BB, can influence the listener's brainwave frequency and are considered effective in enhancing attention and cognitive capabilities. A study on attention discerned that participants listening to BB-Music exhibited superior performance during the test, with attention scores significantly surpassing the control group that didn't listen to BB-Music [2]. Moreover, a growing body of research has converged on similar conclusions, revealing that listening to BB-Music with specific frequency differences can amplify attention in children, university students, and even those with specific psychological disorders [3]. Several investigations have delved into BBMT. For instance, a study by B.K. Isik (2017) ascertained that listening to BB sounds with certain beat frequencies could mitigate stress and anxiety, fostering relaxation and well-being [8]. Furthermore, research by Chaieb et al. (2015) indicated that BB sounds enhance attention, memory, and sleep quality [3]. Thus, BBMT emerges as profoundly efficacious in attention augmentation.

### 2.3   AI Music Generation

In the wake of burgeoning scientific and technological evolution, AI has carved a niche for itself, epitomized by its unparalleled automation and creative prowess [4]. The onset of the "Industry 4.0" wave, compounded with the seismic impact of OpenAI's "ChatGPT" chatbot model, has spotlighted the intersection of AI across diverse disciplines. The innovative amalgamation of AI with music, notably in the realm of AI Music Therapy [16], has magnetized global attention, with prospects looming large. Central to this paradigm shift is the discipline of AI Music Composition, an avenue that seamlessly dovetails music generation into therapeutic vistas [7].

AI Music Composition operates on the premise of sculpting a musical theoretical paradigm via computer algorithms. By curating an array of musical phrase libraries and harnessing machine learning to train specific music style blueprints, it crafts novel digital musical outputs [18]. Delving into its historical trajectory, studies in this domain have a rich tapestry, spanning over thirty years [10]. The MIDI Show Control (MSC) Protocol, instituted by the MIDI Manufacturers Association back in 1991, set the stage for converging focus on AI-facilitated music composition. Pioneering in this domain, JÁNOS KOLLÁR's 2014 exploration gave birth to "Midicine", where MIDI information's musical facets were likened to "medicinal components" [9]. An escalating trajectory of music therapies now harness AI-centric composition tools, encapsulating platforms like Magenta, AIVA, and Amper Music. It's evident that in the realm of AI music genesis, music therapy stands out as a research epicenter, and this inquiry is predicated on exploring BBMT within this expansive landscape.

## 3   Methods

### 3.1   Experiment Objective

This study evaluates the potential of music therapy, particularly AI-generated music, to augment children's attention in comparison to conventional music. Moreover, we integrate BB technology into the musical framework and employ a two-factor mixed experimental design to assess the combined effects of AI music and BBMT on attention enhancement in children.

### 3.2   Experimental Materials

**SNAP-IV Assessment Scale and Music Perception Questionnaire.** The SNAP-IV Assessment Scale is primarily designed to evaluate ADHD and associated behavioral issues. It comprises a version with 26 questions, divided into three sections: attention symptoms, hyperactivity symptoms, and impulsivity symptoms. Each question offers four response options: "Almost Never," "Sometimes," "Often," and "Always." Respondents are required to select answers based on their experiences in the past two weeks. Completion typically takes no longer than 10 min.

The Music Perception Questionnaire contains 8 multiple-choice questions. It quantitatively assesses children's perception of original music, AI music, and the respective BB processed music. The quantified section encompasses eight items: stimulation, liking, acceptance, helpfulness, convenience, continuous use, completeness, and distraction. Each item is rated on a scale from 1 to 5, where 1 indicates "Strongly Disagree" and 5 indicates "Strongly Agree".

The SNAP-IV Assessment Scale is used to identify children with ADD for testing. The purpose of the questionnaire section is to understand children's acceptance levels of the music chosen for this study. After the design of the Music Perception Questionnaire was completed, this study screened 12 ADD children through the SNAP-IV Assessment Scale for a pilot test. The results indicated that the music perception level was moderate, making it suitable for deployment.

**Processing of Original, AI, and BB-Music.** Initially, two popular children's songs were chosen based on play charts and voting results: "YuWoWuGuan" (Pop genre; Bb key; 4/4 rhythm; 63 BPM; 4 min duration) and "GuYongZhe" (Rock genre; G key; 4/4 rhythm; 65 BPM; 4 min and 34 s). To achieve a consistent test duration, both tracks were seamlessly looped to extend to 8 min and 68 s.

Subsequently, to generate AI-derived versions of these songs, we employed Google's Magenta - an open-source AI music generation tool. The AI was trained to replicate the specific scale, beat, tempo, and style of the original songs. The AI-rendered tracks were also adjusted to match the 8-min and 68-s duration, making them compatible with the original tracks for subsequent T-test analyses.

For the integration of the BB technique, the music materials underwent a specific processing method. BB operate by playing two distinct soundwave frequencies to each ear, resulting in a perceived differential frequency within the brain. Based on a study by Zi-Bo Liu (2022) [13], our research selected the $\beta$ wave range (14-30 Hz) for the BB-Music frequency. Using this range, we determined the optimal average beat difference for processing. The general formula for the average calculation is as follows:

$$\text{Aug}_{14-30} = \frac{1}{n} \sum_{i=1}^{n} \chi_i \,, 14 \le \chi_i \le 30 \tag{1}$$

Upon calculation, the average frequency for $\beta$ waves (14–30 Hz) was determined to be approximately 22 Hz. Using this 22 Hz frequency difference, both 8-min and 68-s music tracks underwent processing to incorporate BB with this specific frequency. This process involved infusing each stereo channel of the music with carefully crafted sine waves: the left channel received a 100 Hz frequency, and the right channel a 78 Hz frequency. This configuration effectively generated a BB sound with a frequency of 22 Hz, corresponding to the $\beta$ wave range. Volume adjustments were applied to each channel, and they were subsequently mixed in stereo to create the final BB-Music. The processing of music with BB was used as the within-group variable for comparative analysis.

**Pre and Post-HRV Test.** The HRV pre-test captures baseline heart rate data before the experimental interventions. In contrast, the post-test assesses potential changes across the different groups. Through HRV indicators like SDNN, rmSSD, pNN50, and LF/HF, the T-test is employed to validate the nuances of attention enhancement in children diagnosed with ADD.

**a. SDNN (Standard Deviation of NN intervals):** The SDNN is commonly regarded as an indicator of overall HRV variability. Higher SDNN values suggest increased heart rate variability, which reflects the body's ability to effectively manage stress and emotional fluctuations, often associated with optimal attention levels.

**b. rmSSD (Root Mean Square of Successive Differences):** The rmSSD is an HRV indicator associated with respiratory variability. Higher rmSSD values indicate greater respiratory variability and suggest more robust activity of the autonomic regulatory system, which aligns with an improved attention state.

**c. pNN50 (Proportion of adjacent NN intervals differing by more than 50 ms):** The pNN50 represents the proportion of adjacent heartbeats with intervals exceeding 50 milliseconds. Higher pNN50 values indicate a larger proportion of high-frequency components in heart rate variability, which signifies a favorable balance between the sympathetic and parasympathetic nervous systems, reflecting an optimal attention state.

**d. LF/HF Ratio (Low-Frequency to High-Frequency Ratio):** The LF/HF ratio serves as an equilibrium indicator between sympathetic and parasympathetic nervous system activities. A higher LF/HF ratio implies increased sympathetic activity, while a lower ratio indicates dominance of parasympathetic activity. In a focused state, the LF/HF ratio tends to be lower, indicating a well-balanced interaction between these two systems.

## 3.3  Participants

This study focused on 60 elementary students from Kindergarten A in Taiwan, China, equally divided between males and females. Their ages ranged from 7 to 12 years, averaging at 8 years. After an initial assessment, we selected only those diagnosed with ADD and who had not undergone music therapy before. Participants were then classified based on the music generation method: half were placed in the Original Music (OM) group and the other half in the AI Music (AIM) group. Both groups maintained a gender balance. The research received approval from the Ethics Committee in Taiwan, China. All students participated voluntarily, providing signed informed consent.

## 3.4  Experimental Procedure

As shown in Fig. 1, this study has executed a detailed experimental procedure design. During the preparatory phase, researchers explained the experimental procedure to parents and assisted them in administering the SNAP-IV assessment scale and a music perception questionnaire for their children. Subsequently, the students were divided into two groups, each consisting of 30 participants, based on the results of the SNAP-IV evaluation and the music perception survey.

The study employed a 2 × 2 factorial mixed design, with a focus on the music generation method (an inter-group variable) and the use of BB technology (an intra-group variable). This section led to the creation of the OM group and the AIM group. The HRV tests were divided into one pre-test and two post-tests, conducted after the participants listened to both non-BB treated and BB-treated versions of the music.

Before each HRV test, students were instructed to remain relaxed and avoid vigorous activities. They then listened to the non-BB treated music version via headphones, followed by the first HRV post-test. Subsequently, the BB-treated version of the same music piece was played, concluding with the final HRV post-test. The entire experimental period spanned four weeks, occurring five days a week, with each session lasting 30 min. After each test, the researchers collected the corresponding HRV data from the parents for analysis.

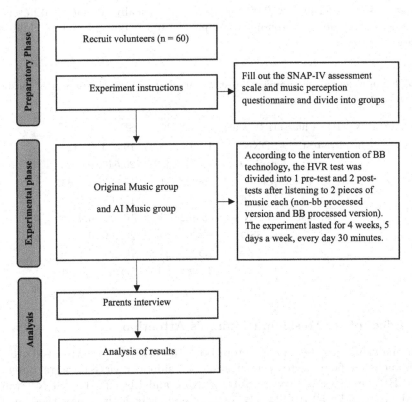

**Fig. 1.** Experiment Procedure Diagram

## 4    Results

This research employed the SPSS (Statistical Package for Social Sciences) tool to scrutinize the outcomes, aiming to discern the amelioration in children's focus when intertwining AI music with BBMT.

### 4.1    Effect of Music on Children's Attention

Utilizing SPSS 26.0, the pre-test and first post-test data from 30 primary school students within the OM group were analyzed. Results revealed improvements in the post-test data across all four HRV indicators: SDNN, rmSSD, pNN50, and LF/HF. The post-test 1 value for SDNN (M = 52.70, SD = 16.522) markedly surpassed its pre-test counterpart (M = 48.03, SD = 16.525). The post-test 1 value for rmSSD (M = 49.64, SD = 23.409) was slightly elevated compared to the pre-test value (M = 49.02, SD = 20.547). The pNN50 value for post-test 1 (M = 28.71, SD = 19.891) was significantly elevated in contrast to the pre-test (M = 21.14, SD = 19.607). On the other hand, the LF/HF ratio for post-test 1 (M = 1.15, SD = 1.507) was marginally diminished relative to its pre-test value (M = 1.39, SD = 1.210). Further validation via an independent sample T-test on data from both groups resulted in P < 0.05, signifying statistically significant differences. This evidence suggests a pronounced impact of music on augmenting children's attention (Table 1).

**Table 1.** An independent samples T-test was used to analyze the impact of music on children's attention.

| N | Test Phase | HRV Data | t | M | SD | P |
|---|---|---|---|---|---|---|
| 30 | Pre-test | SDNN | 12.807 | 48.03 | 16.525 | 0.0122 |
| | | rmSSD | 8.340 | 49.02 | 20.547 | 0.0025 |
| | | pNN50 | 6.892 | 21.14 | 19.607 | 0.0134 |
| | | LF/HF | 6.325 | 1.39 | 1.210 | 0.0244 |
| | Post-test 1 | SDNN | 13.882 | 52.70 | 16.522 | 0.0344 |
| | | rmSSD | 8.836 | 49.64 | 23.409 | 0.0279 |
| | | pNN50 | 7.324 | 28.71 | 19.891 | 0.0259 |
| | | LF/HF | 6.128 | 1.15 | 1.570 | 0.0014 |

### 4.2    Effect of AI Music on Children's Attention

Upon analyzing post-test 1 data from both the original and AI music groups, which included 60 primary school students, minor variations were observed in the HRV metrics: SDNN, rmSSD, pNN50, and LF/HF. The SDNN values of OM group (M = 52.70, SD = 16.522) were slightly higher than those in the AIM group (M = 50.03, SD = 15.612). Conversely, for rmSSD, the OM group

(M = 49.64, SD = 23.409) showed slightly lower values compared to the AIM group (M = 50.01, SD = 24.127). In terms of pNN50, the OM group (M = 28.71, SD = 19.891) exhibited slightly lower values than the AIM group (M = 29.21, SD = 20.007). Furthermore, LF/HF in the OM group (M = 1.15, SD = 1.507) was slightly lower than in the AIM group (M = 1.27, SD=1.725). A paired sample T-test confirmed these observations, with a P-value less than 0.05, indicating statistically significant differences. This underscores that both AI-generated music and traditional original music have a similar effect on enhancing attention in children (Tables 2 and 3).

**Table 2.** A paired-samples T-test was conducted to analyze the effect of AI music on children's attention.

| Group | N | HRV Data | t | M | SD | P |
|-------|---|----------|------|------|------|------|
| OM | 30 | SDNN | 13.882 | 52.70 | 16.522 | 0.0344 |
| | | rmSSD | 8.836 | 49.64 | 23.409 | 0.0279 |
| | | pNN50 | 7.324 | 28.71 | 19.891 | 0.0259 |
| | | LF/HF | 6.128 | 1.15 | 1.570 | 0.0014 |
| AIM | 30 | SDNN | 11.231 | 50.03 | 15.612 | 0.0215 |
| | | rmSSD | 8.125 | 50.01 | 24.127 | 0.0291 |
| | | pNN50 | 8.229 | 29.21 | 20.007 | 0.0315 |
| | | LF/HF | 5.256 | 1.27 | 1.725 | 0.0151 |

**Table 3.** An independent-samples T-test was conducted to analyze the effect of BB-Music on children's attention.

| N | Test Phase | HRV Data | t | M | SD | P |
|---|-----------|----------|------|------|------|------|
| 30 | Post-test 1 | SDNN | 13.882 | 52.70 | 16.522 | 0.0344 |
| | | rmSSD | 8.836 | 49.64 | 23.409 | 0.0279 |
| | | pNN50 | 7.324 | 28.71 | 19.891 | 0.0259 |
| | | LF/HF | 6.128 | 1.15 | 1.570 | 0.0014 |
| | Post-test 2 | SDNN | 15.183 | 60.03 | 17.425 | 0.0213 |
| | | rmSSD | 8.836 | 54.24 | 24.723 | 0.0126 |
| | | pNN50 | 7.324 | 34.31 | 20.128 | 0.0228 |
| | | LF/HF | 6.128 | 1.01 | 1.120 | 0.0076 |

## 4.3    Effect of BB-Music on Children's Attention

Analysis of two post-test sets from 30 primary students in the OM group demonstrated that the post-test 2 data outshone the results from post-test 1 across all HRV indices. The SDNN value from post-test 1 (M = 52.70, SD = 16.522) was notably lower than that of post-test 2 (M = 60.03, SD = 17.425). Similarly, the rmSSD value for post-test 1 (M = 49.64, SD = 23.409) was distinctly lower than for post-test 2 (M = 54.24, SD=24.723). The pNN50 measurement from post-test 1 (M = 28.71, SD = 19.891) was also appreciably lower than from post-test 2 (M = 34.31, SD = 20.128). Yet, the LF/HF ratio for post-test 1 (M = 1.15, SD = 1.507) was marginally higher compared to post-test 2 (M = 1.01, SD = 1.120). The results from an independent sample T-test revealed a statistically significant difference (P < 0.05) between the groups. This confirms that BB-Music has a superior attention-boosting efficacy compared to conventional music.

### 4.4  Effect of Combining AI Music and BB Technology on Children's Attention

An assessment of post-test 2 data from the original and AI music groups, encompassing 60 primary students, showed minimal variations across the HRV metrics. In the OM group, the SDNN value (M = 60.03, SD = 17.425) was significantly greater than in the AIM group (M = 57.54, SD = 16.986). The rmSSD for OM group (M = 54.24, SD = 24.723) was a bit higher than for AIM group (M = 50.72, SD = 23.213). The pNN50 of the OM group (M = 34.31, SD = 20.128) was slightly below that of the AIM group (M = 36.24, SD = 21.198). The LF/HF ratio in the OM group (M = 1.01, SD = 1.120) was somewhat elevated compared to the AIM group (M = 0.97, SD = 1.076). A paired sample T-test, yielding a P-value less than 0.05, affirmed these observations. This indicates that the fusion of AI music with BBMT offers attention-enhancing outcomes on par with traditional BB found in original music (Table 4).

**Table 4.** A paired-samples T-test was conducted to analyze the effect of AI music on children's attention.

| Group | N | HRV Data | t | M | SD | P |
|-------|---|----------|-----|-----|-----|-----|
| OM | 30 | SDNN | 15.183 | 60.03 | 17.425 | 0.0213 |
| | | rmSSD | 8.836 | 54.24 | 24.723 | 0.0126 |
| | | pNN50 | 7.324 | 34.31 | 20.128 | 0.0228 |
| | | LF/HF | 6.128 | 1.01 | 1.120 | 0.0076 |
| AIM | 30 | SDNN | 14.819 | 57.54 | 16.986 | 0.0208 |
| | | rmSSD | 9.157 | 50.72 | 23.213 | 0.0176 |
| | | pNN50 | 8.197 | 36.24 | 21.198 | 0.0179 |
| | | LF/HF | 7.281 | 0.97 | 1.076 | 0.0087 |

## 5  Discussion

### 5.1  Reception to AI Music and BB Treatment

Throughout the research process, qualitative interviews were conducted with both participants and their parents. The findings revealed that both groups demonstrated a high acceptance level for the AI music and BB-Music treatment. An impressive 89% of the participants felt that the AI music content satisfactorily met their listening needs, while 95% believed that the music processed with BB was both more enchanting and comfortable. Observations, in conjunction with feedback from parents, indicated that following the complete experimental procedure, elementary students exhibited enhanced focus on their academic assignments. This was reflected in their elevated efficiency and an observable improvement in the neatness of their written work.

## 5.2    Challenges Encountered in the Experiment

During the course of this research on BB-Music, three primary challenges were encountered. The first challenge pertained to headphones. The comfort of the headphones was paramount; any discomfort could induce anxiety and emotional fluctuations among the schoolchildren, thereby compromising the reliability of the experiment. We explored various options including in-ear Bluetooth headphones, bone conduction headphones, over-ear wired headphones, and over-ear Bluetooth headphones. Based on trials and votes from the participants, over-ear Bluetooth headphones were finally chosen for the study. The second challenge revolved around the selection of a music player. The experiment required a portable music player. Several methods such as mobile phone playback, computer playback, and MP3 playback were tried. Ultimately, Bluetooth headphones equipped with USB data reading capabilities were chosen, enabling the children to directly play music from a USB drive. The third challenge was determining the optimal listening time. Listening during class or physical activity was ruled out, leading us to utilize the 30-min window right before children began their homework post-school. Observations from the experiment highlighted that this listening schedule indeed assisted the students in settling down and efficiently completing their academic tasks.

## 5.3    Limitations and Future Research Directions

This study possesses some inherent limitations that we hope to address in our future research endeavors. The foremost limitation pertains to the universality of the experiment. The music materials used in the experiment were restricted, and the study only incorporated elementary school students as subjects, rendering limited generalizability. Nevertheless, this study sets a preliminary direction for music therapy strategies for ADD. To augment the generalizability of our findings, future endeavors should encompass a broader participant demographic and encompass varied music genres for experimentation. Additionally, our study's scale was somewhat constricted in terms of participant numbers. Hence, to bolster the validity and reliability of our conclusions, future studies should entail larger cohorts. Furthermore, our methodology overlooked potential moderators such as gender, age, and environmental factors which could influence the study's outcomes. Our team aims to delve into these facets in our forthcoming research.

## 6  Conclusion

This research delves into the efficacy of BBMT combined with AI-generated music in enhancing children's attention. Using a $2 \times 2$ factorial design, this study employed a classification of music generation methods and the Brain-Based (BB) technique as between-subjects and within-subjects factors, respectively. Sixty children, approximately 8 years old and diagnosed with Attention Deficit Disorder (ADD) using the SNAP-IV scale, were divided into two groups: Original Music and AI Music, each comprising 30 participants. Both groups underwent intervention with music treated using the BB technique. Heart Rate Variability (HRV) data, analyzed with SPSS, measured attention levels before and after a 4-week intervention, conducted for 30 min a day, five days a week. The results indicated the positive impact of music on enhancing concentration and affirmed the superior effectiveness of the BB technique compared to traditional methods. The combined use of BB and AI music not only enhanced attention but also demonstrated the potential of AI music in therapeutic and regular settings.

**Acknowledgements.** The author sincerely appreciates the steadfast support provided by Shandong Xiehe University (China), Kainan University (Taiwan, China), Kyonggi University (South Korea), Chonnam National University (South Korea), and University Putra (Malaysia) throughout the course of this research.

## References

1. Alda, J.A., Serrano-Troncoso, E.: Attention-deficit hyperactivity disorder: agreement between clinical impression and the snap-iv screening tool. Actas espanolas de psiquiatria **41**(2), 76–83 (2013)
2. Cepeda-Zapata, L.K., Corona-González, C.E., Alonso-Valerdi, L.M., Ibarra-Zarate, D.I.: Binaural beat effects on attention: a study based on the oddball paradigm. Brain Topography **36**, 1–15 (2023)
3. Chaieb, L., Wilpert, E.C., Reber, T.P., Fell, J.: Auditory beat stimulation and its effects on cognition and mood states. Front. Psych. **6**, 70 (2015)
4. Chang, C.Y., Ying-Ping, C.: AntsOMG: a framework aiming to automate creativity and intelligent behavior with a showcase on cantus firmus composition and style development. Electronics **9**(8), 1212 (2020)
5. Draganova, R., Ross, B., Wollbrink, A., Pantev, C.: Cortical steady-state responses to central and peripheral auditory beats. Cerebral Cortex **18**(5), 1193–1200 (2007)
6. Epstein, M.A., Shaywitz, S.E., Shaywitz, B.A., Woolston, J.L.: The boundaries of attention deficit disorder. J. Learn. Disabil. **24**(2), 78–86 (1991)
7. Hamman, M.: On technology and art: Xenakis at work. J. New Music Res. **33**(2), 115–123 (2004)
8. Isik, B., Esen, A., Büyükerkmen, B., Kilinç, A., Menziletoglu, D.: Effectiveness of binaural beats in reducing preoperative dental anxiety. Br. J. Oral Maxillofac. Surg. **55**(6), 571–574 (2017)
9. János, K.: Music therapy for patients with Parkinson's disease. Lege artis medicinae: uj magyar orvosi hirmondo **24**(10–11), 558–560 (2014)
10. Jean-Pierre, B.: From artificial neural networks to deep learning for music generation: history, concepts and trends. Neural Comput. Appl. **33**(1), 39–65 (2021)

11. Kennel, S., Taylor, A.G., Lyon, D., Bourguignon, C.: Pilot feasibility study of binaural auditory beats for reducing symptoms of inattention in children and adolescents with attention-deficit/hyperactivity disorder. J. Pediatr. Nurs. **25**(1), 3–11 (2010)

12. Licklider, J.C.R., Webster, J., Hedlun, J.: On the frequency limits of binaural beats. J. Acoust. Soc. Am. **22**(4), 468–473 (1950)

13. Liu, Z.B., et al.: Short-term efficacy of music therapy combined with $\alpha$ binaural beat therapy in disorders of consciousness. Front. Psychol. **13**, 947861 (2022)

14. Maloy, M., Peterson, R.: A meta-analysis of the effectiveness of music interventions for children and adolescents with attention-deficit/hyperactivity disorder. Psychomusicol. Music Mind Brain **24**(4), 328 (2014)

15. Martin-Moratinos, M., Bella-Fernández, M., Blasco-Fontecilla, H.: Effects of music on attention-deficit/hyperactivity disorder (ADHD) and potential application in serious video games: systematic review. J. Med. Internet Res. **25**, e37742 (2023)

16. Pandey, S.K., Janghel, R.R.: Recent deep learning techniques, challenges and its applications for medical healthcare system: a review. Neural Process. Lett. **50**(2), 1907–1935 (2019)

17. Rajendra Acharya, U., Paul Joseph, K., Kannathal, N., Lim, C.M., Suri, J.S.: Heart rate variability: a review. Med. Biol. Eng. Compu. **44**, 1031–1051 (2006)

18. Roads, C.: Research in music and artificial intelligence. ACM Comput. Surv. **17**(2), 163–190 (1985)

19. Robe, A., Dobrean, A., Cristea, I.A., Păsărelu, C.R., Predescu, E.: Attention-deficit/hyperactivity disorder and task-related heart rate variability: a systematic review and meta-analysis. Neurosci. Biobehav. Rev. **99**, 11–22 (2019)

20. Tonhajzerova, I., et al.: Symbolic dynamics of heart rate variability-a promising tool to investigate cardiac sympathovagal control in attention deficit/hyperactivity disorder (ADHD)? Can. J. Physiol. Pharmacol. **94**(6), 579–587 (2016)

# Generated Therapeutic Music Based on the ISO Principle

Zipeng Qiu[1], Ruibin Yuan[2], Wei Xue[2], and Yucheng Jin[3(✉)]

[1] Fudan University, Shanghai, China
20307130150@fudan.edu.cn
[2] The Hong Kong University of Science and Technology,
Hong Kong SAR, China
ryuanab@connect.ust.hk, weixue@ust.hk
[3] Hong Kong Baptist University, Hong Kong SAR, China
yuchengjin@hkbu.edu.hk

**Abstract.** This paper presents an emotion-driven music generation model designed to support the development of an intelligent system to support music therapy informed by the ISO principle [1]. Following the ISO principle, the system's primary objective is to generate music that aligns with patients' emotions swiftly. To achieve this, we leverage a dataset for emotion recognition to fine-tune a pre-trained audio model, aiding in the annotation of a vast ABC notation dataset. Utilizing these annotated ABC notations, we employ a sequence generation model to build a system that could generate music according to the recognized emotions on the fly, thereby efficiently tailoring musical compositions to the emotional needs of patients in a therapeutic context.

**Keywords:** Music Therapy · Generative Models · Generative Music · Transformer · Autoregressive · Sequence Generation · Emotion Recognition

## 1 Introduction

One of the major tasks for music therapists is to select proper music for patients. However, the music is often selected from the therapists' music library, which may impose several limitations on music selection. First, there is a limit to the variety of music that a therapist can offer. This can be due to their personal knowledge and skills or the lack of resources like musical instruments or recorded music [2]. In addition, it may not always be possible to provide music perfectly tailored to a patient's preferences and emotional state, especially in group therapy sessions [3,4]. Moreover, repeated use of the same music pieces can lead to staleness and reduce the effectiveness of the therapy. However, generative music, created by algorithms, offers a unique and promising approach to music therapy, considering its advantages for personalization, adaptability, and diversity [5,6]. For example, it can adapt to the patient's physiological data or emotional state

X. Li et al. (Eds.): SOMI 2023, CCIS 2007, pp. 32–45, 2024.
https://doi.org/10.1007/978-981-97-0576-4_3

in real-time; and it also can create an infinite amount of unique musical content, making the therapy sessions fresh and engaging for the patients.

In recent years, the popularity of music therapy has witnessed a notable upsurge. Rooted in the ISO principle [1], this therapeutic approach involves patients listening to music that aligns with their current emotional states, followed by a gradual transition towards the desired emotional state through music selection. This practice raises two central inquiries that warrant careful consideration.

The *primary inquiry* pertains to the precise assessment of patients' emotional states. Accurate evaluation of the emotional condition of individuals is crucial to ensure the efficacy of music therapy interventions. The *secondary inquiry* within this therapeutic framework revolves around the music selection that seamlessly aligns with patients' emotional states changing over the period of therapy. This task demands a comprehensive understanding of musical elements and their impact on emotions to ensure that the chosen music resonates with the patients' emotions dynamically.

Measuring human emotions has become a well-established practice in contemporary research. Researchers agree that the two-dimensional framework encompassing valence and arousal constitutes a valid means of assessing human emotion. This framework, originally formulated by Russell [7], has gained empirical support as numerous researchers have demonstrated its simplicity and effectiveness in capturing the complexity of human emotional experiences [8]. Through the utilization of valence-arousal coordinates, a wide spectrum of emotional states can be accurately represented. In recent advancements, researchers have even devised techniques for continuous measurement of valence and arousal utilizing electroencephalography (EEG) [9]. Although these methods offer precision in emotion detection, they necessitate specialized equipment, thus posing challenges for widespread adoption and application.

Music generation encompasses a variety of approaches, each with distinct capabilities. Certain music generation models have the capacity to produce symbolic music in formats such as MIDI [10], subsequently proceeding to synthesize audio from these symbolic representations. On the other hand, some models are capable of directly generating audio [11, 12]. Nevertheless, the majority of these models engage in unconditional generation, rendering them incapable of tailoring musical output to specific emotional contexts. Despite the existence of emotion-based music generation models [10], the relatively long time required for their generation process remains a significant obstacle. This extended generation time does not align with our objectives in developing a music therapy system.

Given the challenges above, the development of a music therapy system incorporating music generation proves to be a difficult task. Consequently, many alternative approaches have been adopted, primarily centering around music recommendation systems [13, 14]. In these systems, a substantial music database is extensively annotated with valence-arousal values or adjective emotion labels. Subsequently, various methods are employed to discern the emotional states of patients. The simplest approach involves directly soliciting emotional feedback from patients. Armed with these emotional values, the recommendation system is then capable of retrieving suitable musical compositions from the annotated database.

Nonetheless, it is worth noting that authentic music therapy can also entail the involvement of live music bands, facilitating improvisational performances. Undoubtedly, such live interventions offer superior therapeutic outcomes compared to the utilization of music recommendation systems. However, it should be acknowledged that the incorporation of live musicians in therapy sessions entails significantly higher costs.

Our objective is to create a music therapy system leveraging music generation models, and in pursuit of this goal, we have devised an innovative approach to address the aforementioned challenges and align with the system's requirements. Our contributions to this endeavor can be summarized as follows:

- We have developed a comprehensive ABC notation dataset that incorporates annotations pertaining to valence-arousal values. This dataset serves as a fundamental resource in our quest to bridge the gap between music generation and emotional context in therapy applications. In our pursuit of a music therapy system rooted in music generation models, we have opted to employ ABC notations as our chosen representation for musical tunes. ABC notations, essentially strings, lend themselves well to training and generation by language models.
- Building upon the dataset, we have engineered a highly efficient music generation model that operates in tandem with valence-arousal values as conditioning factors. Conventional music generation systems are deployed on resource-intensive GPU servers and tend to generate music at a considerably slower speed. In contrast, our streamlined music system can be readily deployed on modestly configured CPU servers, delivering music compositions within a matter of seconds. Therefore, our approach could address the efficiency issue of generating music for therapeutic purposes.
- We have developed a usable and effective music therapy system with a conversational interface to recognize patients' emotional states through dialogue. Subsequently, our music generation system swiftly generates music matching the patients' emotions. This innovative approach ensures that the therapeutic musical experience is tailored to meet the individual emotional needs of each patient, thereby enhancing the efficacy and personalization of the music therapy system.

## 2   Related Work

### 2.1   Emotion-Based Music Generation

Before embarking on this project, extensive testing was conducted on various music generation models. Among them, audio-based music generation models were evaluated [11,12]. Nonetheless, audio generation is often characterized by sluggish performance. Furthermore, a significant drawback of most audio models lies in their unconditional generation nature, rendering them unsuitable for fine-tuning toward emotion-based music generation. Consequently, audio-based outcomes were excluded from consideration in our project.

In contrast, symbolic music encompasses diverse formats, with MIDI being the most prevalent format. Consequently, several symbolic music generation approaches are predicated on MIDI. Additionally, there exists an emotion-based music generation model that the authors introduced in a related paper [10], featuring a symbolic music dataset enriched with continuous valence-arousal labels. Regrettably, this model also suffers from slow generation performance or rough adjustment of emotions, rendering it unsuitable for our specific project objectives.

Symbolic music extends beyond MIDI and includes formats such as music XML and ABC notations, all of which are text-based, facilitating ease of processing within language models. However, music XML's inflexible format, rooted in standard XML structure, presents a challenge, as any textual generation errors may lead to parsing failures. Consequently, few models have ventured into music XML-based generation. In contrast, ABC notations, resembling musical notes, provide a comprehensive representation of musical elements and exhibit greater tolerance towards textual generation errors. As a result, several generation models have been trained on ABC notation datasets, obviating the need for highly specialized design considerations.

Autoregressive models are a staple within the field of Natural Language Processing (NLP) [15]. A basic autoregressive language model proves sufficient for this purpose. The widespread adoption of the Transformer architecture has simplified and empowered text generation, especially when several transformer decoders are connected, allowing for parallel training on large language datasets. This stands in stark contrast to RNN-based models like LSTM and GRU [16,17]. For a project relying on an ABC notation dataset, employing an autoregressive language model like GPT-2 for training suffices, enabling the model to generate musical compositions proficiently [18]. Furthermore, should a conditional generation model be required, using conditions as generation prompts for training becomes a straightforward endeavor. Notably, the utilization of a basic text generation model facilitates efficient deployment on a CPU server, ensuring rapid generation capabilities.

Collectively, these advantages underscore the suitability of ABC notations for our project's requirements. However, the final piece of the puzzle remains obtaining an ABC notation dataset supplemented with valence-arousal annotations to complete the model training process.

## 2.2  Music Dataset with Valence-Arousal Values

Numerous music datasets exhibit considerable diversity in terms of their formats and annotation labels. In this context, there is a pressing need for a dataset characterized by ABC notation paired with valence-arousal labels. Regrettably, such a dataset remains absent from the existing resources. Nevertheless, unlabeled

ABC notation datasets are available. By undertaking the task of annotating select ABC notations with valence-arousal values, we can potentially create a valuable resource for the fine-tuning of pre-trained autoregressive models.

Although most datasets with emotion annotations predominantly employ adjective-based emotional labels [19,20], none of these datasets adhere to the ABC notation format. This discrepancy is primarily rooted in the inherent complexity of conveying arousal through symbolic music, owing to the influence of tempo and timbre synthesized in symbolic music, both of which significantly impact emotional arousal perception.

One notable exception is the EMOPIA dataset [21], renowned for its MIDI format and annotation with the 4Q emotional labels, denoting Low Valence and Low Arousal (LVLA), Low Valence and High Arousal (LVHA), High Valence and Low Arousal (HVLA), and High Valence and High Arousal (HVHA). Even though these labels may not precisely represent valence-arousal values, they offer a marked improvement over adjective-based emotional labels, which inherently suffer from ambiguity in the precise determination of valence and arousal dimensions.

Drawing inspiration from the remarkable success of self-supervised learning paradigms in the field of NLP [15,22], it becomes evident that models trained via self-supervised learning exhibit potent feature extraction capabilities, exemplified by models such as BERT. In the domain of symbolic music, specialized models like MidiBERT and MusicBERT have been developed, tailored specifically for MIDI files [23,24]. However, MidiBERT relies on a MIDI dataset, and MusicBERT presents challenges in terms of fine-tuning, rendering them unsuitable for downstream tasks. Fortunately, pre-trained models are also available in audio formats, such as MERT [25]. A plausible approach involves synthesizing ABC notations into audio representations, thereby enabling the utilization of these audio-based models for further applications.

## 3    ABC Notation Dataset Annotated with Valence-Arousal Values

### 3.1    Methods

Building upon the foundation laid by the previously discussed related work, we propose a standardized approach for dataset construction. Our method is outlined as follows:

- Convert MIDI files in the EMOPIA dataset to WAV files. Then, utilize MERT to fine-tune a 4Q classifier.
- Choose an ABC notation dataset. Then, convert all notations to audio format like WAV.
- Utilize the 4Q classifier to annotate the ABC notation dataset.

Nonetheless, the previously mentioned method is limited in its capacity to annotate ABC notations exclusively with 4Q labels. Drawing inspiration from the converting from categorial label to valence-arousal values approach [26], we propose a novel method that leverages the outputs of the 4Q classifier to rescale label weights into valence-arousal values. Given a WAV sequence denoted as $X$, and considering the 4Q classifier as a function $F_C$, it yields a corresponding 4-dimensional vector, as depicted below:

$$(y_1, y_2, y_3, y_4) = F_C(X) \tag{1}$$

We then transferred it by using the Softmax function.

$$(p_1, p_2, p_3, p_4) = \mathrm{softmax}(y_1, y_2, y_3, y_4) \tag{2}$$

Consequently, by associating low valence and low arousal with a value of $-1$, and high valence and high arousal with a value of 1, we establish direct correspondences between the 4Q labels and their respective valence-arousal values. This allows us to combine these values with the aforementioned weight adjustments, ultimately yielding precise valence and arousal values for the annotated ABC notations. Accordingly, under the assumption that $p_1, p_2, p_3, p_4$ represent the probabilities associated with LVLA (low valence low arousal), LVHA (low valence high arousal), HVLA (high valence low arousal), and HVHA (high valence high arousal), respectively, the resulting valence-arousal values can be calculated as follows:

$$\begin{pmatrix} Valence \\ Arousal \end{pmatrix} = \begin{pmatrix} -1 & -1 & 1 & 1 \\ -1 & 1 & -1 & 1 \end{pmatrix} (p_1, p_2, p_3, p_4)^T \tag{3}$$

We have utilized the Irish Massive ABC Notation dataset (IrishMAN) [27] to implement the aforementioned method, as this dataset supports both MIDI and ABC notation formats, as required for achieving research objectives.

As previously noted, the poor representation of arousal is subject to the nature of symbolic music. In light of this limitation, we have employed density notes as a representation method to capture and represent arousal values within the dataset.

Figure 1 presents the resulting valence and arousal outcomes.

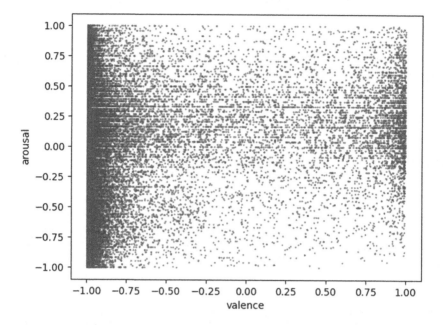

**Fig. 1.** Valence Arousal Distribution

## 3.2   Analysis

Numerous emotion-driven music generation approaches rely on rule-based methodologies. Scientific investigations have affirmed that a range of discernible musical features significantly impact the emotional qualities of music. Notably, distinct musical modes are known to convey different valences. Researchers have demonstrated that the valence of modes such as Phrygian, Aeolian, Dorian, Mixolydian, Ionian, and Lydian tends to exhibit an increasing trend [28].

In the context of ABC notation, it is worth noting that the notation contains a head section marked with "K" that specifies the musical mode. The mode distribution is visually depicted in Fig. 2.

The analysis reveals a notable trend wherein the average valence for each mode aligns closely with the previously established ranking. Nevertheless, it is noteworthy that within each mode, a substantial portion of data clusters around the −1 valence value. This observation suggests that a considerable number of tunes within the dataset exhibit low valence.

This outcome can be attributed to the diversity of musical styles present in the EMOPIA dataset, in contrast to the predominantly classical nature of the Irish dataset. It underscores the idea that musical mode alone is not the sole determinant of valence. Instead, valence appears to be influenced by a multitude of factors inherent to the musical score, which can be challenging to dissect and analyze comprehensively. Consequently, this underscores the importance of training a classifier to assist in the nuanced analysis of these complex musical factors.

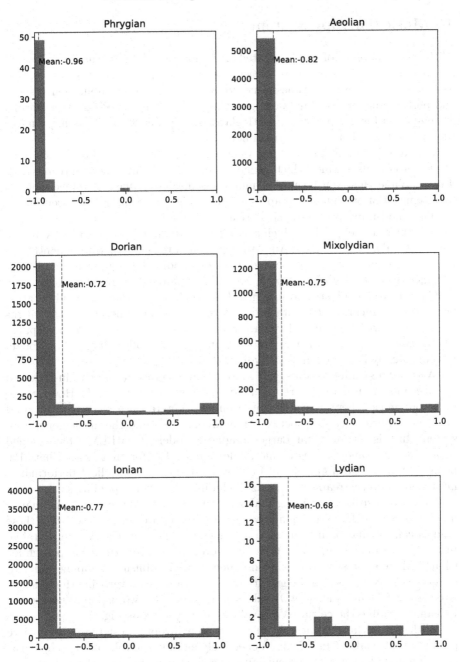

**Fig. 2.** Mode Distributions

# 4  Music Therapy System

With the availability of our annotated ABC notation dataset, the fine-tuning of autoregressive models becomes a feasible endeavor. Among the various options, we have chosen to employ Tunesformer for its advantageous combination of speed and performance in ABC notation generation [27]. Unlike GPT-2, Tunesformer is well-suited for our purposes, particularly in the context of deploying a music therapy system where speed is paramount.

In our fine-tuning process, we take a straightforward approach. We map the valence-arousal scale, which ranges from $-1$ to 1, linearly to integers from 0 to 5. While this transformation maintains discrete values, it suffices for the requirements of our music therapy system, as high precision is not essential.

The fine-tuning process itself is relatively simple. We augment the original Tunesformer model by introducing additional prompts, specifically "V:m" to represent valence $(m)$ and "A:n" to represent arousal $(n)$. Subsequently, we utilize our annotated dataset to fine-tune this modified Tunesformer model.

Once the fine-tuning is complete, the resultant model is capable of generating ABC notations, as illustrated in Fig. 3. It's worth noting that all ABC notation heads can be incorporated into prompts to ensure the generated music aligns more closely with the desired valence rank. In our case, we assume a mapping where valence ranks from 0 to 5 correspond to the modes Phrygian, Aeolian, Dorian, Mixolydian, Ionian, and Lydian, respectively.

With a fine-tuning process, our system can generate music within specified valence and arousal ranges represented by integers from 0 to 5. However, to make our music therapy system more human-centered, we recognize the need for a tool to bridge the gap between human emotions and the music generation system. In this regard, Chat Large Language Models (ChatLLMs) have gained popularity [29], and various online models offer APIs for chat, with ChatGPT being a prominent example. Some of these models exhibit excellent performance in numerous downstream NLP tasks, including zero-shot capabilities.

Our approach involves using dialogues with ChatLLMs to detect and gauge human emotions. However, quantifying valence and arousal directly from these models can be challenging since these values may not be readily interpretable. Instead, we propose employing adjective words as a more intuitive approach for ChatLLMs to express emotions. Consequently, we establish a mapping policy to connect valence-arousal rankings with adjective words by leveraging the Valence, Arousal, and Dominance (VAD) values associated with words [30]. Specifically, we can determine the central VAD values for each rank as Fig. 4.

With the outlined approach, our next step involves designing appropriate prompts that enable ChatLLMs to effectively assume the role of a psychologist, engaging in dialogues with patients and assessing their emotions through conversation. The ultimate objective is to obtain adjective words as descriptors of the patients' emotional states. Here is a prompt example, which is already formatted to JSON as ChatGPT API required.

**Fig. 3.** Generated Music Score with Valence Equals 2 and Arousal Equals 3

```
1   {
2       "role": "system",
3       "content": "You are a helpful psychologist."
4   },
5   {
6       "role": "user",
7       "content": "As a psychologist, your task is to
            engage in a conversation with a patient and
            assess their emotional state. Your response
            should be formatted as JSON, comprising two
            key-value pairs: \"emotion\" and \"response
            .\" For the \"emotion\" key, select an
            adjective that best describes the patient's
            emotion from the following words:\n\n[
            inactivity, weaken, worthless, inaccessible,
            heartache, aggressive, passivity, unoccupied,
             uncherished, sulk, dogged, aggressively,
            passive, overcast, fingernail, kooky,
            challenger, whirlwind, couch, parson,
            sentient, thesis, manifestation, blazing,
            normality, loaf, sensitivity, arise,
            curiosity, euphoric, tranquil, gently, classy
            , approving, phenomenal, excitability]\n\nThe
             \"response\" key should contain your reply
            to the patient's conversation, aimed at
            positively influencing their emotional state
            .\n\nRemember, use pure JSON format to
            response. Do not add any extra words."
```

```
 8  },
 9  {
10      "role": "assistant",
11      "content": "I understand. Now let's start our
            chat. I will return you with the JSON format
            that you require."
12  }
```

This strategy offers several advantages. Firstly, it eliminates the need for the separate fine-tuning of an additional chat model, streamlining the system. Additionally, it leverages the capabilities of commercialized ChatLLMs that provide robust and responsive APIs, reducing the burden of GPU cluster deployment.

By crafting well-structured prompts, we can harness the power of ChatLLMs to engage with users effectively, understand their emotional states, and provide adjective-based descriptions of those emotions, all within the framework of a readily available and accessible platform. This approach not only simplifies the deployment process but also ensures quick and efficient responses to users' emotional needs.

## 5   Discussion

Our research aims to develop an effective music system that could generate therapeutic music according to ISO principles. We employ a pre-trained model to refine a music emotion classifier to achieve this objective. Subsequently, this classifier is used to annotate a dataset with ABC notation. The ensuing annotated dataset is then utilized to fine-tune an autoregressive model. Consequently, the resultant model is adept at generating music in accordance with specified emotional parameters. We propose using LLMs to support the conversational component. Our distinctive contribution is to train a controllable music generation model that follows the ISO principle to generate therapeutic music matching user emotions on the fly.

To the best of our knowledge, our work is the first attempt to leverage an emotion-based music generation model to support the ISO principle. Unlike previous music generation models relying on audio [11,12] or MIDI [10], our model uniquely harnesses ABC notation for emotion-driven music composition. Using ABC notation, a text-based format, could expedite music generation compared to the resource-intensive methods. The simplicity of a GPT structure proves sufficient to fulfill our objective and to enhance the efficiency of the generation process further. We have adopted Tunesformer [27], characterized by its dual-decoder structure, which diminishes attention scale, accelerating the music generation process. This fusion of ABC notation and Tunesformer offers a streamlined and resource-efficient approach to emotion-based music generation.

The ABC notation dataset's annotation assessment relies on a pre-trained model [25] and draws upon a music emotion dataset [21]. However, the accuracy of this annotation proves challenging to ascertain. Given the diverse impacts

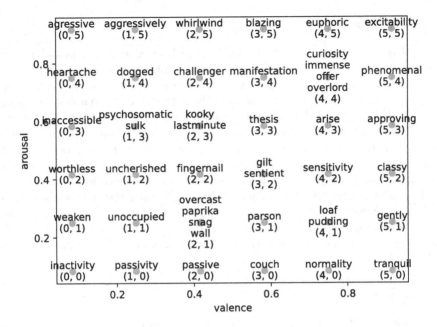

**Fig. 4.** Adjective Words in Valence-Arousal Coordinates

that distinct modes typically exert on individuals, our evaluation centers on analyzing mode distributions. The findings indicate that our annotation broadly aligns with the mode ranking; nevertheless, prevalent low valence predominates. This prevalence suggests the existence of disparate distributions between the EMOPIA dataset [21] and the IrishMAN dataset [27]. Disparities in these distributions may engender inaccuracies in the annotation process. Concurrently, it is imperative to acknowledge the insufficient depth of research in ABC notation synthesis. Presently, numerous ABC notation players remain rudimentary, limited to playing classical instruments. This limitation underscores the need for more comprehensive exploration in the realm of ABC notation synthesis.

In light of the aforementioned limitations, our future research aims to evaluate the effectiveness of the music generation models and the usability of our developed conversational agent equipped with the music generation model. This evaluation will involve the assessment of our system's performance based on users' perceptions of and experience with the generated music. If the system's performance falls short of the desired standards, a potential course of action could involve a paradigm shift in annotation methodology, emphasizing recruiting professionals for annotation purposes. Conversely, should the synthesized output prove unstimulating for the volunteers, an alternative approach may be considered, such as incorporating additional musical elements, including chords and other instruments, to enhance the melodic quality of the tunes. This iterative process is crucial for refining and optimizing the system's performance, ensuring its efficacy within the therapeutic purpose.

## 6    Conclusion

In summary, we have presented a straightforward yet promising approach to construct a music therapy system that leverages annotated ABC notation datasets for fine-tuning autoregressive models. This method offers a cost-effective and accessible way to deploy such a system without the need for complex additional model training. While this approach shows great potential, there are several areas that require further attention. The precision of ABC notation annotations may benefit from the involvement of volunteers and the development of more refined annotation methods. Moreover, the synthesis of ABC notations can be enhanced to address monotony issues, such as the incorporation of chords and diverse instrumentations beyond piano. In our ongoing research, we intend to develop a conversational agent by adopting our method in real-world settings for music therapy. This includes refining the user experience, optimizing the therapeutic effects, and ensuring the practical usability of the system in clinical and everyday contexts.

## References

1. Starcke, K., Mayr, J., von Georgi, R.: Emotion modulation through music after sadness induction-the ISO principle in a controlled experimental study. Int. J. Environ. Res. Public Health **18**(23), 12486 (2021)
2. Beebe, K.: Perceptions of self-determination in music therapy for individuals diagnosed with intellectual disabilities: a survey of music therapists. Music. Ther. Perspect. **40**(1), 94–103 (2022)
3. Baglione, A.N., et al.: Understanding the technological practices and needs of music therapists. In: Proceedings of the ACM on Human-Computer Interaction 5.CSCW1, pp. 1–25 (2021)
4. Wong, H.L.C., Lopez-Nahas, V., Molassiotis, A.: Effects of music therapy on anxiety in ventilator-dependent patients. Heart Lung **30**(5), 376–387 (2001)
5. Carnovalini, F., Roda, A.: Computational creativity and music generation systems: an introduction to the state of the art. Front. Artif. Intell. **3**, 14 (2020)
6. Ji, S., Luo, J., Yang, X.: A comprehensive survey on deep music generation: Multilevel representations, algorithms, evaluations, and future directions. arXiv preprint arXiv:2011.06801 (2020)
7. Russell, J.A.: A circumplex model of affect. J. Pers. Soc. Psychol. **39**(6), 1161 (1980)
8. Schubert, E.: Measuring emotion continuously: validity and reliability of the two-dimensional emotion-space. Australian J. Psychol. **51**(3), 154–165 (1999)
9. Bos, D.O., et al.: EEG-based emotion recognition. Influence Visual Auditory Stimuli. **56**(3), 1–17 (2006)
10. Sulun, S., Davies, M.E.P., Viana, P.: Symbolic music generation conditioned on continuous-valued emotions. IEEE Access **10**, 44617–44626 (2022)
11. Caillon, A., Esling, P.: RAVE: a variational autoencoder for fast and high-quality neural audio synthesis. arXiv preprint arXiv:2111.05011 (2021)
12. Soua, R., Livolant, E., Minet, P.: MUSIKA: a multichannel multi-sink data gathering algorithm in wireless sensor networks. In: 2013 9th International Wireless Communications and Mobile Computing Conference (IWCMC), pp. 1370–1375. IEEE (2013)

13. Ayata, D., Yaslan, Y., Kamasak, M.E.: Emotion based music recommendation system using wearable physiological sensors. IEEE Trans. Consum. Electron. **64**(2), 196–203 (2018)
14. Andjelkovic, I., Parra, D., O'Donovan, J.: Moodplay: interactive mood-based music discovery and recommendation. In: Proceedings of the 2016 Conference on User Modeling Adaptation and Personalization, pp. 275–279 (2016)
15. Radford, A., et al.: Language models are unsupervised multitask learners. OpenAI Blog **1**(8), 9 (2019)
16. Hochreiter, S., Schmidhuber, J.: Long short-term memory. Neural Comput. **9**(8), 1735–1780 (1997)
17. Cho, K., et al.: Learning phrase representations using RNN encoder-decoder for statistical machine translation. arXiv preprint arXiv:1406.1078 (2014)
18. Geerlings, C., Merono-Penuela, A.: Interacting with GPT-2 to generate controlled and believable musical sequences in ABC notation. In: Proceedings of the 1st Workshop on NLP for Music and Audio (NLP4MusA), pp. 49–53 (2020)
19. Bogdanov, D., et al.: MediaEval 2019: emotion and theme recognition in music using Jamendo. In: Larson, M., (eds.) MediaEval'19, Multimedia Benchmark Workshop; 2019 Oct 27–30, Sophia Antipolis, France. Aachen: CEUR; 2019. CEUR Workshop Proceedings (2019)
20. Soleymani, M., et al.: 1000 songs for emotional analysis of music. In: Proceedings of the 2nd ACM International Workshop on Crowdsourcing for Multimedia, pp. 1–6 (2013)
21. Hung, H.-T., et al.: Emopia: a multi-modal pop piano dataset for emotion recognition and emotion-based music generation. arXiv preprint arXiv:2108.01374 (2021)
22. Devlin, J., et al.: Bert: pre-training of deep bidirectional transformers for language understanding. arXiv preprint arXiv:1810.04805 (2018)
23. Chou, Y.-H., et al.: MidiBERT-piano: large-scale pre-training for symbolic music understanding. arXiv preprint arXiv:2107.05223 (2021)
24. Zeng, M., et al.: Musicbert: aymbolic music understanding with large-scale pre-training. arXiv preprint arXiv:2106.05630 (2021)
25. Li, Y., et al.: MERT: acoustic music understanding model with large-scale self-supervised training. arXiv preprint arXiv:2306.00107 (2023)
26. Park, S., et al.: Dimensional emotion detection from categorical emotion. arXiv preprint arXiv:1911.02499 (2019)
27. Wu, S., Sun, M.: TunesFormer: forming tunes with control codes. arXiv preprint arXiv:2301.02884 (2023)
28. Randall, J.K.: Twentieth-Century Harmony: Creative Aspects and Practice (1961)
29. Touvron, H., et al.: Llama 2: open foundation and fine-tuned chat models. arXiv preprint arXiv:2307.09288 (2023)
30. Mohammad, S.: Obtaining reliable human ratings of valence, arousal, and dominance for 20,000 English words. In: Proceedings of the 56th Annual Meeting of the Association for Computational Linguistics (volume 1: Long papers), pp. 174–184 (2018)

# Multimodality in Music

# Utilizing Quantum Particle Swarm Optimization for Multimodal Fusion of Gestures and Facial Expressions in Ensemble Conducting for Emotional Recognition

Xiao Han[1] , Fuyang Chen[1(✉)], and Junrong Ban[2]

[1] College of Automation Engineering, Nanjing University of Aeronautics and Astronautics, Nanjing 210000, China
fuyangchen@nuaa.edu.cn
[2] College of Art, Nanjing University of Aeronautics and Astronautics, Nanjing 210000, China

**Abstract.** The conductor-orchestra interaction is a multimodal process, integrating channels like music, visual cues, postures, and gestures to convey artistic intent accurately. For robots, discerning human emotions from these channels enhances human-machine interaction. Current gesture recognition systems in ensembles prioritize rhythm, tempo, and dynamics; research on the emotional factors of ensembles conducting in music needs to be more extensive. We introduce the Facial Expression and Ensemble Conducting Gesture (FEGE) dataset, comprising eight distinct emotions for recognition. This article presents a Quantum Particle Swarm Optimization Algorithm (QPSO)-based parameter optimization for a Multimodal Fusion Network (QMFN) operating in a multi-feature space, aiming for emotional recognition in dual visual tasks. The network maps conduct facial expressions and gestures into a multi-feature space via dual-modality processing. It learns distinct and shared representations and decodes them using classifiers optimized through QPSO parameters. Experiments on the FEGE dataset validate our network's efficacy. The proposed bimodal fusion network achieves an 83.17% accuracy in dual visual emotion recognition, marking about a 15% enhancement over single-modal recognition results. The proposed method can also be better applied to human-computer interaction systems for ensemble conducting training, aiming to enhance the deeper artistic intent conveyed by the most crucial emotional factors during the conducting process.

**Keywords:** Ensemble Conducting · Quantum Particle Swarm Optimization · Emotional Recognition · Multimodal Fusion Network

## 1 Introduction

In various domains, such as health monitoring, companionship, and life assistance, service robots have showcased their potential, thanks to significant advancements in robotics and artificial intelligence [1]. Particularly in AI, its applications are expanding in fields like music information retrieval, education, therapy, and performance [2]. In the realm of orchestra conducting, Declan Murphy and his team devised a system to manage audio playback through classical techniques. The playback speed is synchronized with gesture beats, mimicking an orchestra's response to a conductor's baton [3]. Besides conveying the dynamics and tempo of music, a conductor's gestures and facial expressions greatly convey the artistic value of a performance [4]. Therefore, recognizing emotions from facial expressions and gestures is crucial in conductor training, particularly in the context of human-robot interactions.

Due to human emotions' complexity, representing them comprehensively using a single modality signal poses challenges. In this work, we introduced the Facial Expressions and Gesture Emotions (FEGE) dataset, encompassing eight discrete emotions tailored for emotion recognition. We developed the Quantum Particle Swarm Optimization Multimodal Fusion Network (QMFN), leveraging a multi-feature space to recognize emotions from facial expressions and gestures. Moreover, we utilized the Quantum Particle Swarm Optimization method to more accurately model the correlations between different modalities, adaptively adjust weights, and hasten convergence. The results indicate that the proposed approach maintains suitability even when one of the modalities is unavailable.

## 2    Related Work

### 2.1    Multimodal Emotion Recognition

With the swift progression of artificial intelligence, emotion recognition, and interpretation have emerged as focal research areas across various domains. Early efforts to discern human emotions primarily utilized individual modalities. However, relying solely on a single modality can result in inaccurate emotional interpretations. Thus, sources beyond the visual modality should be incorporated to enhance emotion recognition. Numerous datasets emphasizing various modalities have been developed for multimodal emotion recognition. Koelstra et al. [5] introduced the DEAP dataset, which pairs positive facial videos with acquired EEG, skin conductance, and ECG data.

### 2.2    Multimodal Fusion Strategies

Multimodal fusion combines information from various modalities and has applications in fields such as emotion analysis, image segmentation, emotion recognition, and individual re-identification [6]. Peña et al. [7] introduced a framework for comparing different fusion methods under the same conditions, which can be used to select the most suitable method for a target task. Furthermore, shared-private learning methods have been explored in multimodal fusion and have shown effectiveness Hazarika et al. [8] and Liu et al. [9] introduced the Cross-Modal Specific Feature Transfer (cm-SSFT) algorithm, aiming to enhance individual re-identification tasks by integrating data from RGB and infrared images. This method effectively integrates shared features to capture cross-modal correlations while obtaining modality-specific features.

### 2.3 Quantum Particle Swarm Optimization

Quantum Particle Swarm Optimization (QPSO) is a variant of Particle Swarm Optimization (PSO) that combines the concepts of quantum computing with the characteristics of the PSO algorithm. Due to the introduction of quantum behavior, QPSO exhibits more robust global search capabilities and can more easily escape local optima. Compared to traditional PSO, QPSO requires fewer parameter adjustments, making it simpler and more efficient in practical applications. QPSO can be applied to various continuous and discrete optimization problems [11].

## 3 FEGE Dataset

### 3.1 Platform and Setup

In the conductor control system for musical ensembles, human emotional states manifest through the interplay of facial expressions and conductor gestures during human-robot interactions. In this study, we used a setup with a USB camera to capture facial expressions and conductor gestures. Participants were guided to exhibit musical emotions through facial expressions and conductor movements synchronized with the music. A controlled relationship between conductor actions and facial expressions for 8 emotions is detailed in Table 1. The USB camera featured a 640x480 resolution and sampled at 25 Hz.

**Table 1.** The Correlation Between Facial Emotions and Conducting Gestures During the Process of Conducting a Musical Ensemble.

| Emotion | Conducting Gestures | Facial Expressions |
|---|---|---|
| Passion-Excitement | Quick and wide arm movements | Bright and lively eyes, possibly wider open Eyebrows might arch up, causing slight forehead wrinkles conveying excitement and tension—corners of the mouth lifting, possibly with a hint of a smile |
| Gentleness-Elegance | Fluid and rounded gestures | Soft and warm gaze, eyes might be slightly narrowed—relaxed eyebrows, a calm forehead without pronounced wrinkles, conveying ease and comfort. The corners of the mouth are slightly upturned, possibly with a smile |

*(continued)*

**Table 1.** (*continued*)

| Emotion | Conducting Gestures | Facial Expressions |
|---|---|---|
| Contemplation-Profundity | Slow and rhythmic gestures | Gaze staring into the distance; eyes might be slightly squinted, indicating introspection and depth. Eyebrows lightly furrowed, a forehead with subtle yet not prominent wrinkles, expressing thoughtful consideration. Lips tightly closed, perhaps slightly upturned |
| Tension-Restraint | Quick, intermittent gestures | Gaze was more focused, eyes slightly widened. Eyebrows slightly furrowed, more wrinkles on the forehead, conveying tension and vigilance. Lips tightly closed, possibly slightly downturned |
| Joy-Delight | Lively and brisk gestures | Eyes squinting into slits, gaze filled with laughter and joy. Eyebrows arching up, a serene forehead conveying pleasure and happiness. Corners of the mouth upturned, with an unmistakable smile |
| Seriousness-Dignity | Stable and powerful gestures | Eyebrows and a composed forehead might slightly furrow, conveying seriousness and concentration. Gaze possibly more concentrated, eyes maintaining a relatively calm state. Lips tightly closed |
| Power-Determination | Strong and forceful gestures | Eyebrows arching up, forehead possibly showing subtle wrinkles, conveying determination and strength. Gaze might become sharper, eyes slightly wider open, displaying energy and resolve. The corners of the mouth might slightly downturn |

(*continued*)

**Table 1.** (*continued*)

| Emotion | Conducting Gestures | Facial Expressions |
|---------|--------------------|--------------------|
| Lyricism-Melancholy | Gentle and flowing gestures | Eyebrows might slightly arch up or downturn, and the forehead might have delicate wrinkles. Gaze might become gentler, eyes possibly slightly moist. Lips might slightly downturn |

## 3.2 Data Acquisition

The experiment was carried out in a soundproof room with a laptop and a previously mentioned video recording system. Two cameras beside the computer recorded participants' facial expressions and gestures. To ensure authentic emotional responses, participants underwent the experiment five times, interacting with six unique music excerpts randomly. Participants conveyed emotions from music excerpts through gestures and facial expressions, yielding bimodal data for each emotion per experiment (a trial). The FEGE dataset comprises 300 dual-modal samples containing facial videos and conducting gesture data. The video data is recorded as a series of JPG images in the RGB color space. Each image has a resolution of $640 \times 480$ pixels.

## 3.3 Data Processing

We employed a multitask cascaded convolutional network to track and extract image data from each recorded video frame. The dimensions of facial images were adjusted to $224 \times 224$ pixels. To crop the data, we selected the earliest start time and the latest end time for each facial-conducting gesture dual-modal data pair and cropped the data along the time dimension. After data cropping, redundant frames from the dual-modal task data pairs were eliminated. Figure 1 illustrates the duration comparison of facial expressions and conducting gestures across the eight different emotions.

We selected both data streams' earliest start and latest end times for each facial-gesture dual-modal data pair. For real-time recognition, we segmented each data pair into sub-samples of duration d, overlapping by d/2, as shown in Fig. 1. Duration d was defined as 1 s, corresponding to a 25-frame visual sequence. For sub-samples shorter than d, the last frame's data was padded. Three sub-samples were selected for emotion recognition, primarily for two reasons. First, the initial data's emotional features are distinct. Second, utilizing all sub-samples results in significant class imbalance. Ultimately, we obtained 579 data pairs for emotion recognition.

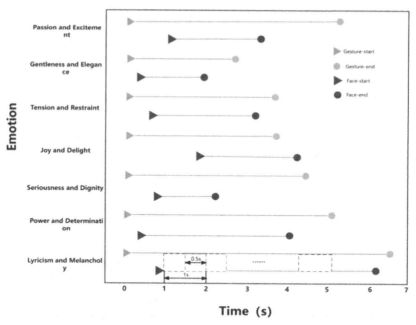

**Fig. 1.** In the FEGE dataset, the average duration of facial expressions and directive gesture actions for eight emotional states (triangular symbols represent the start time, circular symbols represent the end time).

## 4  Proposed Method

In order to better integrate facial and gesture double visual task modalities, a Multimodal Emotion Recognition (MER) framework was proposed, as illustrated in Fig. 2. This framework consists of four components:

1. Feature extractors for each visual modality
2. Subspace feature encoders for each visual task modality
3. Shared feature encoders for both visual task modalities
4. Three classifiers, each designed to handle a specific set of features related to different modalities, and one classifier for the shared features across modalities.
5. Joining learning based on Quantum Particle Swarm Optimization

The description outlines the emotion recognition problem based on directive conducting gestures and facial expressions. We utilize a dual-modal training dataset encompassing two different data types. Represented as $D_g = \left[ x_g^1, x_g^2, ..., x_g^N \right] \in \mathbb{R}^{N \times w_g \times h_g \times t_g}$ and $D_f = \left[ x_f^1, x_f^2, ..., x_f^N \right] \in \mathbb{R}^{N \times 3 \times w_f \times h_f \times t_f}$, denoting facial and gestural samples, respectively, with N indicating the number of training samples encompassing both facial and gestural data. Additionally, $t_u$ and $t_v$ represent the quantity of sampled frames for gestures and facial expressions, while $w_g \times h_g$ and $w_f \times h_f$ denote the spatial resolutions. Furthermore, since the facial-gesture samples share the same sampling frequency, the frame counts $t_u$ and $t_v$ are identical. Each facial-gestural sample pair is assigned emotion label $y \in \mathbb{R}^c$, where C represents the number of emotion categories. The objective is to develop a resilient classifier that can effectively predict emotional labels based on facial expressions and directive gestures.

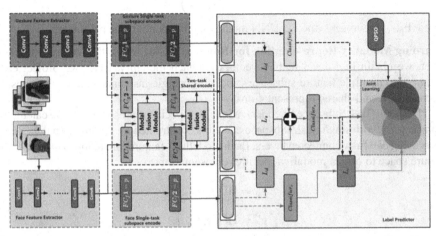

**Fig. 2.** The proposed QMFN framework can be summarized as follows. QMFN consists of feature extractors, single-task subspace encoders, a shared encoder, and a joint learning module based on Quantum Particle Swarm Optimization (QPSO). The single-task subspace and shared encoder are designed to learn modality-specific and modality-invariant representations, respectively. The Quantum Particle Swarm Optimization algorithm optimizes parameters efficiently, while the joint learning module constructs specific invariant subspaces and trains the classification boundaries.

## 4.1 Main Modules

**The Ensemble Conducting Gesture Network.** Conductor gestures collected from a camera involve both the visual appearance of the body shape and dynamic motion. Effectively modeling spatiotemporal features using video sequences can enhance emotion recognition performance. Our research employed a Convolutional Neural Network (CNN) in 3D to extract spatiotemporal features from the raw gesture sequences. The emotion recognition network for conductor gesture actions can be represented as shown in Eq. (1), provided with a set of conductor gestural samples $x_g$.

$$f_g = F_g(x_g, \theta_{F_g}) \tag{1}$$

In this context, $f_u$ represents the features extracted from $x_g$, $F_g(\cdot, \cdot)$ denotes the CNN in 3D, and $\theta_{F_g}$ signifies the associated parameters.

**Ensemble Conducting Facial Expression Network.** The facial expression network records facial expression data, including shape appearance and temporal dynamics. It effectively models spatiotemporal features using video sequences. 3D CNN has been effectively employed for spatiotemporal feature extraction and facial expression recognition [10]. As a visual network, the 3D CNN model, pre-trained on the sports-1 dataset, is employed for extracting facial expression features [11]. Equation (2) represents the features extracted from the visual network, denoted as fv, for a batch of facial expression samples xf.

$$f_f = F_f(x_f, \theta_{F_f}) \tag{2}$$

where $F_f(\cdot, \cdot)$ represents the 3D CNN model, and $\theta_{F_f}$ denotes the parameters.

**Learning Modality Representation for Bimodal Tasks.** After the feature extraction layer, we obtain high-level feature vectors for each modality. Here, we project each feature into multiple feature subspaces, including single-task and shared subspaces, to learn specific and shared representations.

(1) Single-Task Subspace Encoders: Modality-specific representations are calculated using Eq. (3), with single-task subspace encoders constructed for various visual modality tasks using two fully connected layers. Each modality's features are mapped to its specific feature space to obtain modality-specific representations.

$$g_g^p = H_g^P\left(f_g, \theta_{H_g}^p\right)$$
$$g_f^p = H_f^P\left(f_f, \theta_{H_f}^p\right) \tag{3}$$

Here, $H_g^P$ and $H_f^P$ represent the command gesture task subspace encoder and the facial task subspace encoder, respectively, with their respective parameters denoted as $\theta_{H_g}^p$ and $\theta_{H_f}^p$; $g_g^p$ and $g_f^p$ represent the specific features for the command gesture modality task and the facial modality task, respectively.

(2) Shared Encoder: In the shared encoder, we aim to acquire common representations across various modalities within a unified subspace by leveraging distributed similarity constraints. This approach enables us to reduce heterogeneity gaps. Figure 2 illustrates the utilization of two separate fully connected layers to create encoders Ψ_1 and Ψ_2, which share a common structure but do not have parameter sharing with encoders Φ_h and Φ_f. The mathematical representation of the shared encoder's operation is depicted in Eq. (4).

$$g_g^s = H_g^s\left(f_g, \theta_{H_g}^s\right)$$
$$g_f^s = H_f^s(f_f, \theta_{H_f}^s) \tag{4}$$

Here, $H_g^s$ and $H_f^s$ represent the subnetworks for facial visual and gesture visual task modalities within the shared encoder, with their respective parameters denoted as $\theta_{H_g}^s$ and $\theta_{H_f}^s$. $g_g^s$ and $g_f^s$ represent the output features of $H_g^s$ and $H_f^s$ respectively.

A multimodal fusion module has been devised to rectify the disparities in data formats across various visual modality tasks, effectively mitigating the heterogeneity between features $g_g^s$ and $g_f^s$. Figure 3 describes the specific operations within the multimodal fusion module.

Assuming $g_g^s \in \mathbb{R}^{d_g}$ and $g_f^s \in \mathbb{R}^{d_f}$, we first need to obtain a joint representation $J \in \mathbb{R}^{d_J}$ based on $g_g^s$ and $g_f^s$ in Eq. (5).

$$J = \omega\left[g_g^s, g_f^s\right] \tag{5}$$

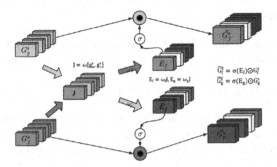

**Fig. 3.** The Architecture of Bimodal Fusion Modules for Two Task Modalities.

Where $g_g^s$, $g_f^s$, and J denote the feature dimensions of $d_g$, $d_f$ and $d_j$ the joint representation respectively, and r is a positive constant greater than 1, often used to control model capacity and enhance generalization ability. Activation signals are determined via two layers, as in Eq. (6), using symbols $[\cdot, \cdot]$ for concatenation and $\omega \in \mathbb{R}^{d_g \times d_f}$ for weight.

$$E_g = \omega_g J, E_f = \omega_f J \tag{6}$$

In the fully connected layers, $\omega_g \in \mathbb{R}^{d_g \times d_j}$ and $\omega_f \in \mathbb{R}^{d_f \times d_j}$ represent the weights. Following this, $E_g$ and $E_f$ are used to recalibrate the specific input features, as depicted in Eq. (7).

$$\begin{aligned}\widetilde{g_g^s} &= \sigma(E_g) \odot g_g^s \\ \widetilde{g_f^s} &= \sigma(E_f) \odot g_f^s\end{aligned} \tag{7}$$

Here, $\sigma(\cdot)$ represents the sigmoid function, and $\odot$ denotes the element-wise multiplication operation.

**Classifier.** In our research, rather than computing a joint representation for specific and shared features, we built three classifiers for three types of features. This ensures that the method can continue to function effectively even if one of the modality tasks is missing. The operation of the classifiers is represented in Eq. (8).

$$\begin{aligned}O_g &= C_g\big(g_g^p, \theta_{c_g}\big) \\ O_f &= C_f\big(g_f^p, \theta_{c_f}\big) \\ O_s &= C_s\big([\widetilde{g_u^s}, \widetilde{g_v^s}], \theta_{c_s}\big)\end{aligned} \tag{8}$$

Classifiers $C_g$, $C_f$, and $C_s$ are for gestures, faces, and both. They label $O_u$, $O_v$, and $O_s$ with parameters $\theta_{c_g}$, $\theta_{c_f}$, and $\theta_{c_s}$. Training adjusts parameters for emotion detection. In testing, results, o, match Eq. (9).

$$\begin{cases} (o_g + o_f + o_s)/3, & \text{All available modalities} \\ o_f, & \text{Omission of facial modality} \\ o_g, & \text{Omission of gestural modality} \end{cases} \tag{9}$$

## 4.2  Joint Learning

By referencing the outcome of Eq. (12) and the genuine labels y from Eq. (10), we deduce the classification loss $L_c$ (illustrated by the orange-red shape in Fig. 2).

$$L_d = \mathbb{E}_{x_g \in \mathfrak{D}_g} J(o_g, y) + \mathbb{E}_{x_f \in \mathfrak{D}_f} J(o_f, y) + \mathbb{E}_{x_g, x_f \in \mathfrak{D}_g, \mathfrak{D}_f} J(o_s, y) \tag{10}$$

$J(\cdot,\cdot)$ is the cross-entropy loss, showing classifier risk. Minimizing it sets decision boundaries. For a shared representation from face-command gestures, we reduce feature distances. Similarity loss $L_s$ (in light green in Fig. 2) is in Eq. (11).

$$L_S = \left\| \tilde{g}_g^s - \tilde{g}_F^s \right\|_F^2 \tag{11}$$

where $\| \cdot \|_F^2$ signifies the squared measure of the Frobenius norm. By reducing this, the joint attributes from the face-command gesture dual tasks converge to a singular space, wiping out mode-based variances and securing a collective depiction. Aiming for unique and non-duplicative attributes, we push for encoders, both shared and exclusive, to interpret different inputs via a divergence loss influencing both types. As a result, for the orthogonal mapping of shared and distinct attributes for every type, the divergence loss $L_d$ (showcased by the amber figure in Fig. 2), aligns with Eq. (12).

$$L_s = \left\| \tilde{g}_g^{s^T} \tilde{g}_g^s \right\|_F^2 + \left\| \tilde{g}_f^{s^T} \tilde{g}_f^s \right\|_F^2 \tag{12}$$

By minimizing $L_d$, we aim to orient shared and exclusive traits more orthogonally, enabling the acquisition of representations for each standalone task type. Given the losses before, the target function for the proposed model is captured in Eq. (13).

$$L(\Theta) = L_c + \alpha L_s + \beta L_d \tag{13}$$

Here, $\alpha$ and $\beta$ serve as the collection of model parameters and also indicate the coefficients for the similarity loss and divergence loss, respectively. $\Theta$ encompasses $\{\theta_{F_g}, \theta_{F_f}, \theta_{H_g}^p,$ $\theta_{H_f}^p, \theta_{H_g}^s, \theta_{H_f}^s, \theta_{C_g}, \theta_{C_f}, \theta_{C_s}, \omega, \omega_g, \omega_f\}$, and the adjustments to these parameters are guided by Eq. (14).

$$\hat{\Theta} = \arg \min_{\Theta} (\Theta) \tag{14}$$

## 4.3  Quantum Particle Swarm Optimization-Based Parameter Optimization for Joint Learning in Multimodal Data Fusion

Multimodal data fusion integrates various sensor information to yield accurate and comprehensive insights. Utilizing Quantum Particle Swarm Optimization (QPSO) offers benefits like enhanced exploration of diverse data spaces, identifying optimal fusion solutions, and thorough exploration of multimodal data combinations. In gesture-facial dual-visual data fusion, modality correlations and weights may vary over time or with environmental changes. QPSO effectively adapts to these fluctuations. Traditional optimization struggles with the curse of dimensionality in high-dimensional spaces. Conversely, QPSO outperforms in high-dimensional optimization, allowing efficient exploration of intricate data spaces. QPSO's optimization process facilitates information crosstalk and fusion among visual modal tasks, yielding comprehensive fusion results. In the Joint Learning process, parameters such as estimation metrics, similarity loss weights, and dissimilarity loss weights need configuration. QPSO can efficiently configure these parameters, eliminating manual adjustments. The QPSO process includes: 1) Parameter initialization. 2) Fitness function computation for each particle. 3) Updating local and global bests. 4) Parameter updates per Eq. (15). 5) Repeating steps 2–4 until meeting stopping criteria. The program flowchart of the QPSO model is summarized in Algorithm 1.

In order to expedite the evaluation process, numerous methods have been proposed [13]. A hybrid algorithm is constructed as follows: firstly, a random subset of the dataset is chosen for parameter optimization. Secondly, the stability (S) of candidate solutions (candidate parameter values) is calculated based on the following formula (15):

$$S = \mu/\sigma, \text{Where } \mu = \sum_i^N c_i^k/N \text{ and } \sigma = \sqrt{\sum_i^N \left(C_i^k - \mu\right)^2/N} \qquad (15)$$

C represents the accurate classification obtained from candidate parameters, while N denotes the number of solutions. Thirdly, if the performance of the solutions is relatively stable, there is no need to continue the training process, thus prematurely terminating the current iteration rounds. The selected parameter set will be forwarded to the Joint Learning module for sentiment classification of bimodal visual tasks in the test dataset. A detailed description of QMFN can be found in Table 2.

---

**Algorithm 1** Integration of QPSO into Joint Learning Algorithm

1: **Input:** Training dataset, learning rate $\mu$, maximum number of iterations $E$, hyperparameters $\alpha, \beta$
2: **Output:** Predicted labels for the samples in the testing dataset $o$
3: Initialize quantum particle swarm $P$ (including position, velocity, and other quantum attributes)
4: Evaluate the fitness of the initial particle swarm $P$ (using objective function)
                                  ▷ Single-modal optimization phase
5: **for** $k = 0, 1$ **do**
6:     **for** $iter = 1$ to $E$ **do**
7:         Update the positions of particle swarm $P$ focused on modality $k$'s parameters via QPSO
8:         Evaluate the fitness of particles at new positions
9:         Update the best particle and global best particle (if fitness improves)
10:     **end for**
11: **end for**
                                ▷ Initialize multi-modal parameters $\Theta$
12: Extract parameters from the global best particle to initialize $\Theta$
                                ▷ Multi-modal optimization phase
13: **for** $iter = 1$ to $E$ **do**
14:     Update the positions of particle swarm $P$ focused on overall multi-modal parameters $\Theta$ via QPSO
15:     Evaluate the fitness of particles at new positions
16:     Update the best particle and global best particle (if fitness improves)
17: **end for**
                                   ▷ Output Predictions
18: Extract optimal parameters $\Theta$ from global best particle
19: Return predicted labels $o$ using optimal parameters $\Theta$ and Eqs. (8) and (9)

**Table 2.** QMFN architecture in our experiments.

| Stage | Filters | | |
|---|---|---|---|
| | Facial network | Shared network | Gestural network |
| Conv1 | $\begin{bmatrix} 1 \times 3 \times 1, 128 \\ 1 \times 1 \times 3, 4 \\ 3 \times 1 \times 1, 32 \end{bmatrix} \times 1$ | - | $[3 \times 3 \times 3, 64] \times 1$ |
| Conv2 | $\begin{bmatrix} 1 \times 3 \times 1, 512 \\ 1 \times 1 \times 3, 32 \\ 3 \times 1 \times 1, 128 \end{bmatrix} \times 1$ | - | $[3 \times 3 \times 3, 128] \times 1$ |
| Conv3 | $\begin{bmatrix} 1 \times 3 \times 1, 1024 \\ 1 \times 1 \times 3, 128 \\ 3 \times 1 \times 1, 256 \end{bmatrix} \times 1$ | - | $[3 \times 3 \times 3, 256] \times 2$ |
| Conv4 | $\begin{bmatrix} 1 \times 3 \times 1, 1024 \\ 1 \times 1 \times 3, 256 \\ 3 \times 1 \times 1, 256 \end{bmatrix} \times 1$ | - | $[3 \times 3 \times 3, 512] \times 2$ |
| Conv5 | $1$ | - | $[3 \times 3 \times 3, 512] \times 2$ |
| FC1 | $1 \times 1 \times 1, 64$ | - | $1 \times 1 \times 1, 4096$ |
| FC2 | $1 \times 1 \times 1, 64$ | $1 \times 1 \times 1, 64$ $1 \times 1 \times 1, 64$ | $1 \times 1 \times 1, 64$ |
| Cat | - | $1 \times 1 \times 1, 128$ | - |
| FC3 | $1 \times 1 \times 1, 6$ | $1 \times 1 \times 1, 6$ | $1 \times 1 \times 1, 6$ |

## 5 Experimental Results and Analysis

### 5.1 Emotion Recognition Results

To compare the performance of different fusion methods in bimodal emotion recognition for command gestures and facial expressions, we selected the following methods as baseline comparisons:

(1) Single Modality: C3D and d3D, as previously noted, were trained for gestures and facial tasks.
(2) Feature Fusion: C3D and d3D extracted emotion features. Early fusion used concatenation, CBP, and TFN [13].
(3) Decision Fusion: C3D and d3D predicted emotion probabilities. Fusion methods were averaging multiplication and Mulmix [14].

(4) Model Fusion: Model Fusion: ECFCEG, MMTM, and MSAF fused command gestures and faces".

Recognizing emotions through command gestures and facial cues outperforms methods based on a single modality. In the realm of bimodal emotion detection using command gestures and facial cues, our suggested technique stands out with the top accuracy among all multi-modal fusion strategies. Table 3 presents the outcomes of performance comparisons. As indicated in Table 3, our approach registers accuracy and F1 scores that are 4.84% and 4.66% superior to the leading model-based fusion technique.

**Table 3.** The performance comparison of various models on the FEGE Dataset.

| Standards | Models | Evaluation metrics | |
|---|---|---|---|
| | | ACC (%) | F1 Score (%) |
| Singe Gesture | d3D | 66.01 | 64.28 |
| Singe Face | C3D | 64.05 | 62.75 |
| Feature Fusion | Concatenation | 75.23 | 73.10 |
| | CBP [16] | 74.79 | 71.14 |
| | TFN [15] | 75.68 | 73.80 |
| Decision Fusion | Averaging | 73.07 | 70.47 |
| | Multiplication | 74.35 | 70.80 |
| | Mulmix [17] | 75.17 | 70.64 |
| Model Fusion | MMTM [5] | 76.51 | 74.82 |
| | MSAF [18] | 77.89 | 73.67 |
| | ECFCEG [19] | 78.33 | 74.23 |
| | QMFN | 83.17 | 78.89 |

Utilizing QMFN brings forth several performance enhancements. Initially, the amalgamation of unimodal and multimodal classifiers for emotion discernment provides a heightened level of trust compared to their solo operations. Moreover, the act of honing the similarity loss counteracts modal mismatches, thus uplifting the outcomes of multimodal classifiers. In contrast, fine-tuning the diversity loss ensures the retention of unique modal characteristics, and purging any repetitive elements bolsters the results of single-mode classifiers. The fusion technique for dual modes, primarily when centered on shared attributes in command gestures and facial indicators, aids in forging a standard feature set, pushing the performance envelope further.

For an in-depth evaluation, we delved into confusion matrices to gauge emotion identification across modalities such as ensemble task, ensemble facial task, feature merging (using concatenation), decision amalgamation (by averaging), model integration (F-CCA-PLI), and our innovative QMFN, illustrated in Fig. 4. Figures 4(a) and (b) highlight that within the gesture-centric modality, emotions like Passion and Excitement reached an apex in accuracy at 88.0%, whereas Contemplation and Profundity lagged at

41.3%. Transitioning to the facial-centric modality, emotions like Joy and Delight led the pack with 79.3% accuracy, while Gentleness and Elegance lagged at 40.1%. Notably, the emotion pairs often misinterpreted differed between the gesture and facial modalities. In the gesture-focused realm, the trio of most interchanged emotion pairs comprised Seriousness and Dignity with Contemplation and Profundity (30.0%), Joy and Delight with Contemplation and Profundity (29.1%), and Gentleness and Elegance with Seriousness and Dignity (28.0%). Conversely, in the vision-focused realm, the predominant interchanged pairs were Contemplation and Profundity with Tension and Restraint (60.0%), Gentleness and Elegance with Seriousness and Dignity (37.0%), and Seriousness with Delight and Contemplation and Profundity (28.0%). This accentuates the distinct capabilities of gesture and vision-based modalities in identifying a spectrum of emotions, reiterating the supplementary insights gestures offer in emotion discernment.

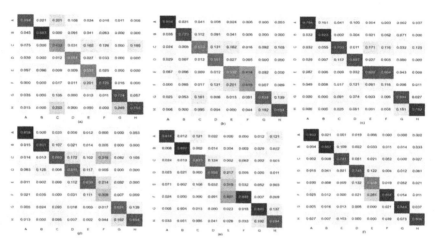

**Fig. 4.** Confusion matrices for command gestures and facial expressions based on (a) Gesture modality, (b) Facial modality, (c) Concatenation, (d) Averaging, (e) MISA, and (f) QMFN. In these matrices, each letter corresponds to the following emotions: A - Joy and Delight, B - Passion and Excitement, C - Contemplation and Profundity, D - Tension and Restraint, E - Gentleness and Elegance, F - Seriousness and Dignity, G - Power and Determination.

Figures 4(c) and (d) highlight that, against the backdrop of singular modality techniques, feature fusion approaches underscore a marked uptick in the accuracy of classifying emotions, notably Passion, Excitement-Tension, and Restraint. Contrarily, decision fusion mechanisms amplify the precision in discerning emotions like Sadness and Fear. Furthermore, feature fusion tactics register significant advancements for the emotion that lags in performance (Gentleness and Elegance) within command gestures and facial indicators. On the contrary, decision fusion methods bolster the identification of emotions with heightened classification across modalities but wield a lesser influence on suboptimally classified emotions. An encompassing evaluation posits that feature and decision fusion paradigms harbor distinct strengths in multi-modal emotion identification, suggesting avenues for refining classification outcomes.

Figure 4(e) depicts that, compared to unimodal techniques, QMFN registers notable enhancements in the precision of classifying emotions like Power and Determination. Analogous advancements are evident for other emotional categories when set against feature and decision fusion approaches.

Figure(f) shows that QMFN achieves superior performance on the FETE dataset and all the emotion categories have an accuracy higher than 50%, whereas the classification accuracies of happiness and sadness show great improvements. In addition, the emotion misclassification reduces greatly among all the methods.

## 5.2   Ablation Analysis and Discussion

The inaugural row showcases the classification outcomes for the full-fledged QMFN model. The subsequent row omits the Quantum Particle Swarm Optimization segment. The third and fifth rows exclude the diversity loss, similarity loss, and the combined loss metrics from the model. We executed a sequence of ablation tests to investigate the impact of various elements and loss metrics within our suggested framework. These outcomes are tabulated in Table 4. The comparative analysis underscores that the most pronounced dip in performance arises when the similarity loss is excluded.

**Table 4.** Results of ablation experiments.

| Method | Evaluation metrics | |
|---|---|---|
| | ACC (%) | F1 score(%) |
| QMFN | 83.17 | 78.89 |
| w/o QPSO | 80.16 | 78.51 |
| w/o $L_s$ | 77.63 | 74.25 |
| w/o $L_d$ | 75.53 | 73.55 |
| w/o $L_s+L_d$ | 76.12 | 74.23 |
| w/o fusion Module | 76.08 | 73.97 |
| w/o fusion Module, and $L_s+L_d$ | 75.23 | 73.10 |
| w/o Classifier$_u$ and Classifier$_v$ | 75.23 | 73.10 |
| w/o Classifier$_s$ | 73.07 | 70.47 |

Omitting the similarity loss perturbs both private and shared encoding mechanisms, culminating in a notable loss of semantic essence in shared and unique attributes. On the other hand, discarding the diversity loss exerts a minimal influence on the model's efficacy. This stems from the intertwined learning dynamics of diversity and similarity losses, which inherently clash. The diversity loss's exclusion does not impinge on the private encoder in the context of the similarity loss. When these loss metrics are sidelined, the model reverts to a composite learning structure pivoted on facial and gesture visual tasks coupled with feature amalgamation networks. These trio of ablation studies accentuate the pivotal role of communal learning and distinct attributes within QMFN.

The penultimate row discards the multimodal fusion component, leading to a 4.1% dip in precision. This fusion element bridges modal variances and paves the way for a unified feature domain. This trial highlights the indispensable function of the multimodal fusion facet in QMFN. Conclusively, with the backdrop of sidelining diversity, similarity losses, and the multimodal fusion component, the last two rows phase out specific and communal classifiers. The outcomes from these dual ablation studies rank the lowest, signifying QMFN's reliance on integrating multiple classification mechanisms.

## 6    Conclusion

In this work, we unveiled a pioneering multimodal emotion recognition approach, QMFN, anchored on the Quantum Particle Swarm Optimization (QPSO) algorithm and affirmed its effectiveness through the FEGE dataset. In this endeavor, we curated a dataset for facial and gesture visual tasks, termed the FEGE dataset, encapsulating eight varied emotional categories, thereby enhancing the adeptness in discerning emotions from orchestral conductors' facial expressions and conducting gestures. The formulated QMFN harnesses unique and communal representations from assorted modalities, integrating a spectrum of classifiers for adept emotion identification. Additionally, the insights gleaned indicate that the amalgamation of facial and gesture dual visual task modalities significantly bolsters the efficacy of emotion recognition. Empirical analyses affirm the robustness of QMFN in bifocal emotion recognition concerning facial expressions and conducting gestures. Nonetheless, the expansion in modalities amplifies the QMFN's structural complexity and computational demands, steering future investigations toward the development of lean multimodal fusion architectures.

**Availability of Data and Material.**    All raw data is available from the authors.

**Disclosure of Interests.**    The authors have no competing interests to declare that are relevant to the content of this article.

## References

1. Hong, A., et al.: A multi-modal emotional human-robot interaction architecture for social robots engaged in bidi-rectional communication. IEEE Trans. Cybern. **51**(12), 5954–5968 (2021)
2. Han, X., Chen, F., Ullah, I., Faisal, M.: An evaluation of AI-based college music teaching using AHP and MOORA. Soft Comput. 1–11 (2023). https://doi.org/10.1007/s00500-023-08717-5
3. Murphy, D., Andersen, T.H., Jensen, K.: Conducting audio files via computer vision. In: Ges-ture-Based Communication in Human-Computer Interaction: 5th International Gesture Work-shop, GW 2003, Genova, Italy, pp. 529–540 (2004)
4. Patrikov, G.: Pedagogical problems of working on rhapsodic fantasy by dimitar nenov in the curriculum in orchestra conducting by piano. Knowl. Int. J. **28**(3), 1051–1056 (2018)
5. Koelstra, S., et al. "Deap: A database for emotion analysis; using physiological sig-nals." IEEE Trans. Affect. Comput. **3**(1), 18–31 (2011)

6. Heredia, J., et al. "Adaptive multimodal emotion detection architecture for social ro-bots." IEEE Access 10, 20727–20744 (2022)

7. Peña, D., et al. "A Framework to Evaluate Fusion Methods for Multimodal Emotion Recognition." IEEE Access 11, 10218–10237 (2023)

8. Hazarika, D., Zimmermann, R., Poria, S.: Misa: modality-invariant and-specific representations for multimodal sentiment analysis. In: Proceedings of the 28th ACM International Conference on Multimedia, pp. 1122–1131 (2020)

9. Liu, S., Reviriego, P., Montuschi, P., Lombardi, F.: Error-Tolerant computation for voting classifiers with multiple classes. IEEE Trans. Veh. Technol. **69**(11), 13718–13727 (2020)

10. Dong, Y., Zhao, L.: Quantum behaved particle swarm optimization algorithm based on artificial fish swarm. Math. Probl. Eng. **2014**, 592682 (2014). https://doi.org/10.1155/2014/592682

11. Zhang, L., Gui, G., Khattak, A.M., Wang, M., Gao, W., Jia, J.: Multi-task cascaded convolutional networks based intelligent fruit detection for designing automated robot. IEEE Access **7**, 56028–56038 (2019)

12. Tran, D., Wang, H., Torresani, L., Ray, J., LeCun, Y., Paluri, M.: A closer look at spatiotemporal convolutions for action recognition. In: Proceedings of the IEEE Conference on Com-puter Vision and Pattern Recognition, pp. 6450–6459 (2018)

13. Tran, D., Bourdev, L., Fergus, R., Torresani, L., Paluri, M.: Learning spatiotemporal fea-tures with 3d convolutional networks. In: Proceedings of the IEEE International Conference on Computer Vision, pp. 4489–4497 (2015)

14. Wang, B., Sun, Y., Xue, B., Zhang, M.: Evolving deep convolutional neural networks by variable-length particle swarm optimization for image classification. In: 2018 IEEE Congress on Evolutionary Computation (CEC), pp. 1–8 (2018)

15. Zadeh, A., Chen, M., Poria, S., Cambria, E., Morency, L. P.: Tensor fusion network for multimodal sentiment analysis. arXiv preprint (2017). https://doi.org/10.48550/arXiv.1707.07250

16. Nguyen Tien, D., Nguyen Thanh, K., Sridharan, S., Dean, D., Fookes, C.: Deep spatiotemporal feature fusion with compact bilinear pooling for multimodal emotion recognition. Comput. Vis. Image Underst. **174**, 33–42 (2018)

17. Liu, K., Li, Y., Xu, N., Natarajan, P.: Learn to combine modalities in multimodal deep learning. arXiv preprint arXiv:1805.11730 (2018). https://doi.org/10.48550/arXiv.1805.11730

18. Su, L., Hu, C., Li, G., Cao, D.: Msaf: Multimodal split attention fusion. arXiv preprint arXiv: 2012.07175 (2020). https://doi.org/10.48550/arXiv.2012.07175

19. Sun, X., Zheng, X., Li, T., Li, Y., Cui, L.: Multimodal emotion classification method and analysis of brain functional connectivity networks. IEEE Trans. Neural Syst. Rehabil. Eng. **30**, 2022–2031 (2022)

# Guqin Jianzi Notation Transcription Based on Language Model

Kaiwen Shi[1], Kan Liu[1]([✉])[iD], and Xizi Zhang[2]

[1] Zhongnan University of Economics and Law, Wuhan, China
shikaiwen@zuel.stu.edu.cn, liukan@zuel.edu.cn
[2] Wuhan Conservatory of Music, Wuhan, China

**Abstract.** Guqin is an intangible cultural heritage of China. The jianzi notation is the music notation reduced from the written notation, which does not contain clear note duration and rhythmic information. Translating the Guqin jianzi notation into modern sheet music means transcription, which is time-consuming. There are more than 3,000 jianzi notations in existence, but only a hundred or so can be played. If use the playable jianzi notations to train the transcription model, it is expected to revitalize a large number of jianzi notationa of the Guqin. In this paper, we define the transcription process as the duration annotation of the jianzi sequence, and construct a notation duration prediction model for Guqin jianzi notation under the limited number of existing playable Guqin notations. Firstly, based on the deconstruction of Guqin jianzi, a method is designed to deconstruct jianzi, and the jianzi containing fingering information are split into left, right, hui and string. Then, the jianzi language model QinBERT is constructed to fit the deconstructed jianzi, and the embedding layer of the language model is expanded for the deconstructed jianzi. Finally, the validation study of the duration prediction of Guqin jianzi notation is carried out on a manually collected dataset containing 54 Guqin songs. The duration prediction model based on the jianzi language model has the best performance among the comparison experiments, and the size of the vocabulary of the deconstructed jianzi language model is about 1/4 of that of the baseline model.

**Keywords:** Jianzi Notation · Notation Transcription · Language Model · Duration Prediction

## 1 Introduction

Among the traditional Chinese folk instruments, the Guqin has a unique notation. The earliest pieces of Guqin music were recorded entirely in words, called written notation, which contains the fingers used by the player, the string and

The research is supported by Fundamental Research Funds for the Central Universities "Research on Guqin Jianzi Notation Transcription Based on Language Model" (202351411), Zhongnan University of Economics and Law.

hui [1], and the player's expression. The jianzi notation, which is a reduced version of the written notation, is a record of the left and right fingerings used in playing, and the corresponding string and hui. String and hui of Guqin are shown in Fig. 1. The jianzi notation only records the way of playing, but not the exact duration of each note, so a piece of jianzi notation can not be played directly. It is necessary to describe the rhythm and pitch of the piece by using modern music notation, which is a notation transcription process and is called "da pu". Transcription requires the musicians to gather extensive information, and often consumes a great deal of time. However, of the more than 3,000 pieces of Guqin jianzi notations that have been handed down, only a hundred or so can be played by contemporary musicians.

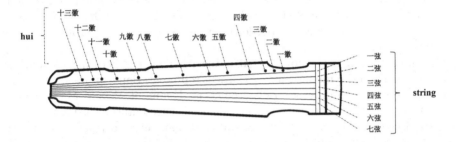

**Fig. 1.** Diagram of Guqin Structure.

In 1989, Chen [1] mentioned in the literature that "the research of Guqin musical heritage (including jianzi notation transcription) has traditionally been carried out by the 'human brain', and whether it can be assisted by the 'computer brain' is worth studying". There are two difficulties for computer-assisted Guqin transcription. One difficulty lies in the duration prediction, the composition of jianzi is numerous. Another difficulty lies in the fact that the number of existing pieces that can be played is limited, which is difficult for language model training.

Aiming at the problem of duration prediction, this paper will model the jianzi symbol system with language model, and the learning paradigm of pre-training plus fine-tuning is used to realize the duration prediction of the notes in the musical transcription. Aiming at the problem of small-scale corpus, this paper adds fingering information to the jianzi notation data, constructs Guqin jianzi notation dataset with fingering information. At the same time, based on the characteristics of Guqin jianzi, we design a method to deconstruct jianzi, which reduces the size of the language model vocabulary to 1/4 of the original one. Based on the deconstructed jianzi, the language model is designed to fully express the pitch and movement information of various combinations of jianzi words, and ultimately improve the effect of Guqin transcription.

---

[1] Similar to stringed instruments such as guitar and violin, the Guqin's hui is used to adjust the pitch of the instrument as it is played.

## 2    Related Works

With the development of computer technology, researchers applying information technology to the study of Guqin music. The research on digitization of jianzi notation for Guqin mainly focuses on theory and analysis of jianzi notation. The work of jianzi notation digitization mainly discusses how to encode the jianzi notation, so as to facilitate the representation of jianzi notation in the computer [2–6]. Research on jianzi notation analysis is mainly centered on using data mining algorithms to analyze the content of jianzi notation in combination with music theory [7–13]. Among them, Li et al. constructed a Guqin music dataset containing 71 jianzi tunes and performed pitch analysis on this dataset, but the fingering information of jianzi notation was not recorded [13]. It is worth mentioning the most recent research that related to jianzi notation digitization: Wei and Wang [14] contribute the world's first Ch'in Tablature character dataset, and proposed a novel method in order to translate Guqin jianzi from images to digital version.

Inspired by language modeling in natural language processing techniques, early research on symbolic music learned representations of music symbols through contextual music notation prediction. Huang et al. and Madjiheurem et al. treated chords as words and learned chord representations using word2vec [15,16]. Herremans et al. and Chuan et al. and Liang et al. divided musical segments into non-overlapping musical segments with fixed durations and trained embeddings for each segment [17–19]. Tatsunori et al. grouped musical notes and considered these groups of notes as words for representation learning [20]. As pre-trained language models have been well studied, the work of Tsai et al. represents the first attempt to use pre-trained models for symbolic music classification [21]. In recent years, Chou et al. proposed MidiBERT and carried out research work on pre-training music language models on 4166 MIDI files [22]. Zeng et al. also proposed MusicBERT using data in MIDI format for pre-training [23]. After pre-training using more than one million multi-track MIDI musical compositions, MusicBERT was applied to two generative music tasks and two sequence-level discriminative tasks. Unlike MusicBERT, which is capable of handling multi-track MIDI data, MidiBERT can only handle single-track piano MIDI data. Wang et al. proposed MuseBERT in 2021, which improves positional encoding for context-dependent musical relationships [24].

The above studies of Guqin show that the encoding rules of jianzi notation are not uniform, and is various from job to job. Since the jianzi notation is numerous, but the existing playable notations are limited. With the development of natural language processing technology, studies on music language modeling bring a new way to Guqin transcription research. This paper proposes a deconstructed jianzi method that contains fingering information and a language model of jianzi to realize Guqin jianzi transcription, in which the fingering information is represented in the form of text. And proposes to reduce the model's demand for training data by decreasing the size of the jianzi vocabulary, so that it can effectively complete the computer-assisted transcription.

# 3  Dataset

## 3.1  Jianzi Notation Dataset Construction

In order to extract more semantic information from the jianzi notation and enrich the Guqin music dataset, this paper supplements fingering information as a new feature for the conventional Guqin music data. The existing datasets about Guqin music do not contain fingering information, which requires manual entry of jianzi fingering and the time value of each note. Since Li et al. constructed a dataset of Guqin pitches on Guqin music collections with simplified notations [13], these notations are widely accepted versions of Guqin music, which are the standard versions for teaching and playing. In this paper, a total of 54 pieces [25,26] were selected from these Guqin notation collections, and undergraduate student majoring in Guqin at the Conservatory of Music carried out the work of entering jianzi notation data. In this way, the dataset contains a total of 22,196 jianzi, 2,331 combinations of jianzi, and 12 types of note durations. The distribution of jianzi notation lengths and the distribution of the number of note types are shown in Fig. 2, where "*" and "-" in the note duration types denote dotted notes and sustained lines, respectively.

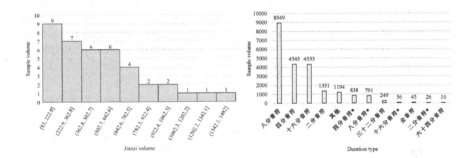

**Fig. 2.** The Distribution of Jianzi Notation Length and Notation Duration Type.

Figure 3 illustrates some selections from the notation of "Feng Qiu Huang", taking the third and fourth bars as an example, which will be converted to the following text during data entry: "食指七徽勾四弦，八分音符\n勾五弦，八分音符\n挑七弦，八分音符*\n勾六弦，十六分音符\n挑七弦，四分音符\n泛止，其他\n \n散勾六弦，八分音符\n大指七徽六分勾七弦，四分音符-\n剔七弦，八分音符\n大指九徽抹七弦，八分音符\n上七徽六分，八分音符\n大指九徽挑七弦，八分音符\n无名指十徽起\n \n".

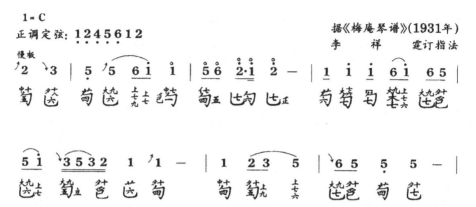

Fig. 3. Excerpts from The Notation of Guqin Song "Feng Qiu Huang".

## 3.2 Special Jianzi Encoding

Each notation is saved in a text file, and each line of the file records a pair of jianzi and the note type. Figure 4 lists the three categories of special jianzi cases encountered in the data entry process, and different entry strategies are adopted for different categories of jianzi combination cases according to the principle that one movement corresponds to one note.

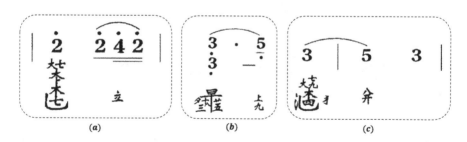

Fig. 4. Examples of Three Types of Special Jianzi.

Example (a) is entered as "大指七徽抹七弦，四分音符\n挑七弦，八分音符\n进，十六分音符\n复，十六分音符\n\n". For the combined jianzi of the "抹挑" fingering, replace it with the separate jianzis of "抹" and "挑". For the jianzi "撞", split it into "进" and "复" jianzi, so that one jianzi can correspond to one note.

Example (b) is recorded as "撮无名指十徽八分三弦散五弦，四分音符*\n上九徽，八分音符". In this example, the two jianzi correspond to two sets of note types, and if "撮" is recorded as "四分音符-", then "上九徽" does not correspond to any note. Therefore, if "撮" is recorded as "四分音符*", then both jianzi correspond to one note, which is in line with the logic of the movement during the playing process.

Example (c) is recorded as "大指七徽九分抹四弦，四分音符\n猱，其他\n\n上七徽，四分音符\n挑七徽九分四弦，四分音符\n\n". In Guqin playing, the "分开" fingering is usually combined with "抹挑" or "勾剔", and corresponds to three movements. Therefore, according to the logic of playing, it can be broken down into three jianzi.

## 4    Methodology

### 4.1    Workflow

The construction of the duration prediction model is divided into 3 steps: data sampling and process, jianzi language model pre-training and duration prediction model training, and the workflow is shown in Fig. 5.

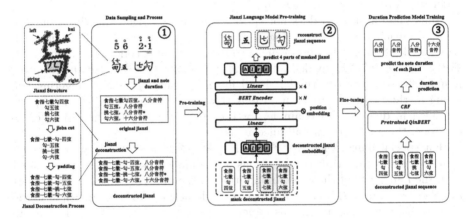

**Fig. 5.** The Workflow of Guqin Jianzi Notation Transcription.

The core idea of the model in this paper is to view the problem of predicting the note durations of Guqin jianzi notation as a sequence labeling problem. One or more jianzi will correspond to one or more left and right hand movements, so not every jianzi corresponds to a note. From the point of view of computer-assisted transcription: if the sequence annotation method is used, the problem of multiple jianzi corresponding to a single note can be solved by simply introducing a new category label. For example, for the sequence of jianzi: "食指七徽勾四弦，勾五弦，挑七弦，勾六弦，挑七弦，泛止", to predict the sequence of note types: "八分音符，八分音符，八分音符*，十六分音符，四分音符-，其他".

In the stage of data sampling and process, the music data are collected and reviewed manually, and the fingering information of jianzi and the duration of the corresponding notes are recorded into the text file; then, the jianzi in the data are deconstructed according to the components of the fingering. In the pre-training stage of the jianzi language model, the deconstructed jianzi sequence without labeling information are masked to obtain the pre-training dataset, and the pre-training of the language model (named QinBERT in this paper) is completed by predicting the masked jianzi positions. In the training stage of the duration prediction model, the pre-trained QinBERT is fine-tuned with a CRF layer to predict the note duration corresponding to each jianzi.

## 4.2 Jianzi Deconstruction

The jianzi, which contains fingering information, consists of four parts: left, right, hui and string, as shown in Fig. 5 stage 1. Guqin has 7 strings, 13 hui, and dozens of left and right, and the free arrangement constructs numerous jianzi. If the jianzi is directly input as a model, the complexity of the vocabulary will be very large, and it is difficult for the language model to learn the relationship between individual jianzi from the limited corpus. In this paper, we deconstruct jianzi, which requires only the left, right, hui and string to be determined in order to express the playing action.

Since the initial data does not specify the left and right fingerings, hui and string for each jianzi, a fingerings dictionary is constructed and the jianzi is segmented into words to obtain the deconstructed jianzi code. For example, "大指七徽九分挑四弦" is divided into "大指-七徽九分-挑-四弦", and the resulting four parts correspond to the left hand fingering, hui, right hand fingering and string in the code. For jianzi notations that are not fingerings, the four parts are filled in directly. For example, for the cue "泛起" at the beginning of an overtone, the four parts are all filled in as "泛起".

For special jianzi, such as "撮无名指十徽八分三弦散五弦", after the split word, we will get multiple combinations of movements, which are not consistent with the four parts of the code. In addition to the fingering method "撮", there are also "拨" and "剌", etc., in which a single action produces multiple notes. To cope with this situation, this paper simplifies these special jianzi, and fills all four parts of the code with right-hand fingering because it represents how to pluck the strings, which is more representative of the playing action. The method of deconstructing jianzi is allowed to handle all jianzi while preserving as much fingering information as possible.

As shown in Table 1, there are 2,331 undeconstructed jianzi, 557 deconstructed jianzi tokens in the vocabulary, which is about 23.8% of the size of the original vocabulary. This deconstruction method can reduce the vocabulary of the language model, thus reducing the corpus needed for pre-training of the language model.

**Table 1.** Distribution of Deconstructed Jianzi

| Jianzi Type | Jianzi | Left | Right | String | Hui |
|---|---|---|---|---|---|
| Volume | 2331 | 92 | 177 | 126 | 162 |

## 4.3   Jianzi Language Model

Due to the uniqueness of Guqin jianzi, there is no language model trained based on Guqin jianzi corpus. This paper proposes a language model for Guqin jiazi named QinBERT. As shown in the Fig. 5 stage 2, the backbone structure of the QinBERT model adopts the BERT module, which expands the word embedding part of the BERT to include the left, right, hui, and string, and then the four embedding vectors are added together and fed into a fully connected layer. After jianzi embedding, relative position embedding vector is added to the word embedding vectors in order to introduce the sequence position information, and then they are fed into several BERT modules for feature extraction. After feature extraction, the output vectors of the BERT hidden layer are fed into each of the four fully connected layers to predict the masked part.

When training the jianzi language model, we randomly mask some of the jianzi in the input sequence and predict the masked jianzi. Since Guqin jianzi notation exists in a cis-recording, random masking will lead to cis-information leakage if the proposed jianzi coding in this paper is used. Therefore, the same set of jianzi representations is considered as a unit and masked at the same time, which can avoid information leakage, and a better contextual representation can be learned through pre-training.

## 4.4   Notation Duration Prediction

Since the jianzi notation note duration prediction task is defined as a sequence labeling task, directly classifying the activation values of the hidden layer of QinBERT may result in a misordering of the labeling logic, leading to the sudden appearance of fast-paced phrases in the middle of a passage with a gentle tempo. In order to avoid this situation [14,28], a CRF layer is added on top of QinBERT, thus composing the QinBERT-CRF transcription model, and the model structure is shown in Fig. 5 stage 3.

When training the QinBERT-CRF duration prediction model, the cross-entropy loss between the activation value $H = (H_1, H_2, ..., H_n)$ of the QinBERT hidden layer and the note temporal value type labels $Y = (Y_1, Y_2, ..., Y_n)$ can be computed by Eq. (1).

$$loss = -\sum_{i=1}^{n} Y_i \log(H_i) \tag{1}$$

The activation value $H$ of the hidden layer is input into the CRF layer and the conditional probability $P(Y|X)$ can be calculated by Eq. (2).

$$P(Y|X) = softmax(\sum_{i,k} \lambda_k t_k (Y_{i-1}, Y_i, H, i) + \sum_{i,l} \mu_l s_l (Y_i, H, i)) \tag{2}$$

where $t_k$ and $s_l$ are the characteristic functions, $\lambda_k$ and $\mu_l$ are the corresponding weights. The process of calculating the conditional probability $P(Y|X)$ is a probability-maximizing optimal path solving problem, and the predicted labels of the note tensors can be derived by the Viterbi algorithm.

## 5    Experiments and Result Analysis

### 5.1    Experiment Setup

Different players have different styles of handling melodic rhythms, and the determination of duration is a kind of creation in itself, so there is no right or wrong in scoring, but only an aesthetic difference in art. On the basis of the language model of jianzi notation, the jianzi notation in Guqin jianzi notation is disassembled into different fingering parts, which form the jianzi notation, and the jianzi notation constitutes the music score. In order to investigate the correlation between each fingering, jianzi and the rhythm of the piece, this paper designed a comparison experiment, an embedding layer role analysis experiment and a data volume experiment.

In the experimental process, firstly, the manually collected data were verified, and after correcting the errors, jieba was utilized to segment the jianzi to obtain the deconstructed jianzi dataset. In pre-training, the music samples were masked with 15% jianzi at a time, and 80% of the masked jianzi were replaced with [MASK], 10% were replaced with random elements, and 10% were kept unchanged. QinBERT hidden layer size is 256 and self-attention head is 8. QinBERT is pre-trained for 10 epoches, learning rate and batch size is $2e-5$ and 128. In fine-tuning stage, the model is trained for 200 epoches, the learning rate is $1e-4$ and the batch size is 64. The experiment uses Precision, Recall, F1, and Accuracy to evaluate the performance of the duration prediction model.

### 5.2    Comparison Experiment Analysis

The comparison experiment mainly compares the model of this paper with the deep learning methods, and the combination of classical word vector models Word2Vec and GloVe with different encoders BiLSTM and BERT is set as a control. QinBERT with different number of layers and different hidden layer dimensions are also added in the experiments to find the number of model parameters adapted to the current data volume. The experimental results are shown in Table 2.

From the experimental results, the performance of the model using static word vectors is generally poor, and the F1 value of the model is around 0.5. On the one hand, static word vectors themselves are not expressive enough; on the other hand, jianzi is directly used as a model input, and the encoder's learning space is very large. Compared with the static word vector model, QinBERT can achieve better performance, with F1 values and accuracy above 0.6, which is the best result of the current research about computerized transcription. However, with the increase of the depth and width of the model, the performance of transcription is not significantly improved. This indicates that the knowledge learned by the model is basically saturated, and the increase in the number of parameters will not generate new knowledge.

**Table 2.** Results of Comparison Experiment

| Method | Precision | Recall | F1 | Accuracy |
|---|---|---|---|---|
| Word2Vec +BiLSTM | 0.4821 | 0.5570 | 0.4647 | 0.5570 |
| Word2Vec+BERT | 0.5363 | 0.5647 | 0.5442 | 0.5647 |
| GloVe +BiLSTM | 0.4770 | 0.5407 | 0.4585 | 0.5407 |
| GloVe+BERT | 0.5262 | 0.5545 | 0.5366 | 0.5545 |
| 4 layers QinBERT | 0.6352 | **0.6408** | **0.6194** | **0.6408** |
| 6 layers QinBERT | 0.6373 | 0.6262 | 0.6037 | 0.6262 |
| 6 layers QinBERT(768) | 0.6371 | 0.6332 | 0.6011 | 0.6332 |
| 12 layers QinBERT | **0.6495** | 0.6352 | 0.6140 | 0.6352 |

The above analysis suggests that the use of jianzi after deconstruction is more effective for note duration prediction. For the language model, the deconstruction of Guqin jianzi reduces the number of embedding vectors that need to be learned, and the free combination of jianzi can better express the information contained in the original jianzi; for the jianzi transcription, the results of the comparative experiments corroborate Lin's view that "as the main body of jianzi notation, it also has the function of indicating rhythm in addition to indicating the method of playing" [27]. The combination logic of different jianzi characters can reflect the process of music performance, and the better prediction effect of the deconstruction of jianzi characters indicates that the combination of jianzi characters contains the rhythmic combination of Guqin performance.

## 5.3   Jianzi Embedding Analysis

There are 4 embedding layers in the QinBERT language model, the 4 parts of jianzi fingerings will be deleted one by one to analyze the role of each embedding layer on the duration prediction. The experiment is conducted using 4-layer QinBERT, and the results are shown in Table 3.

Overall, the feature input of the deconstructed jianzi-based character encoding proposed in this paper performs best in the task of duration prediction. The gradual deletion of the embedding layer leads to a degradation of the model performance, indicating the effectiveness of the character encoding in this paper for the character characterization of jianzi.

From the perspective of Guqin performance, the hui and string sequence of a jianzi character can express the pitch information, and the combination of the string sequence and the left and right can constitute the movement information. In the grouping with one and two layers deleted, the model containing the hui and string sequences performs relatively well, which indicates that the incorporation of pitch information can enhance the rhythmic delineation of the transcription. In the grouping of deleting the three layers, the model of retaining the string, right and hui achieved the best F1 value, Recall and Precision within the grouping. It is noteworthy that the model that retains only the hui embedding also performs

**Table 3.** Results of Jianzi Embedding Layer Analysis Experiments

| Input | Precision | Recall | F1 | Accuracy |
|---|---|---|---|---|
| All | 0.6352 | 0.6408 | 0.6194 | 0.6408 |
| hui, left, right | 0.5466 | 0.5680 | 0.5265 | 0.5547 |
| hui, left, string | 0.5023 | 0.5534 | 0.5265 | 0.5349 |
| hui, right, string | 0.5909 | **0.5825** | **0.5420** | 0.5798 |
| left, right, string | **0.6352** | 0.5534 | **0.5420** | **0.5850** |
| right, string | **0.5909** | 0.5680 | 0.5265 | **0.5696** |
| left, string | 0.5613 | 0.5534 | 0.5265 | 0.5548 |
| left, right | 0.5613 | 0.5534 | 0.5265 | 0.5548 |
| hui, string | 0.5023 | **0.5825** | **0.5420** | 0.5500 |
| hui, right | 0.4727 | 0.5389 | 0.4800 | 0.5041 |
| hui, left | 0.4875 | 0.5243 | 0.5265 | 0.5202 |
| string | 0.5909 | 0.5534 | **0.5575** | **0.5754** |
| right | 0.5761 | **0.5680** | 0.4955 | 0.5539 |
| left | 0.6057 | 0.5243 | 0.5420 | 0.5653 |
| hui | **0.6204** | 0.5534 | 0.5110 | 0.5693 |

better in Precision and Accuracy. Whereas the hui express the pitch information of the piece, the sequence of hui expresses how the pitch of the piece changes. This suggests that the pitch change information can indicate the rhythm of the piece to a certain extent, while the model with only the hui information did not perform better because: among the three timbres played by Guqin, only the presses and overtones use the hui, and only the right hand is used in the performance of the scattering tone, so it is difficult to predict the rhythm of the scattering tone by only providing the hui information.

The results of the above ablation experiments also show that the embedded expressions generated by the language model are consistent with the logic of Guqin performance, while the jianzi without any part of the word are unable to express the logic of the music performance.

### 5.4   Data Volume Analysis

The data volume experiments explored whether or not the combination of jianzis would contain rhythmic information that would be beneficial for duration prediction from the perspective of the transcription. The data volume experiments were pre-trained and fine-tuned using 4-layer QinBERT. The effect of data volume on model performance is observed by adjusting the proportion of samples invested in training.

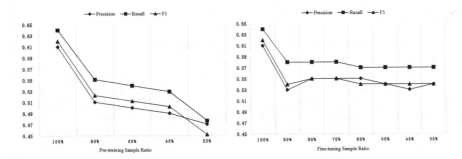

**Fig. 6.** Relationship between Pre-training Sample Size (left), Fine-tuning Sample Size (right) and Model Performance.

As shown in Fig. 6, as the amount of data continues decreasing, the performance of the model with missing data in the pre-training phase decreases faster, while the missing data in the fine-tuning phase has less impact.

The results of the data volume experiments show that, in addition to the jianzi notations themselves indicating the musical rhythm, the combinations of jianzi notations also contain rhythmic patterns. As the number of training samples increases, the model is able to learn more rhythmic patterns, and is also able to apply these patterns to different pieces of music. This suggests that the determination of the rhythm of Guqin music can not only start from the information indicated by the jianzi characters themselves, but also mine similar rhythms or variations from the perspective of the combination of jianzi characters. For example, in a piece like *Three Melodies of Plum Blossoms* or *Three Folds of Yangguan*, there are several recurring melodies. These melodies have similar jianzi correspondences and are similar in essence in terms of their playing logic, with the exception of the position of the presses or overtones in the left.

# 6   Conclusion

This paper centers on computerized transcription for Guqin, defining computer-aided transcription as a sequence annotation task. The key work of this paper is to design a new encoding method for jianzi notation data, and deconstruct the jianzi combination through the method of word splitting, in order to reach the purpose of reducing the complexity of the word list, which effectively improves the training efficiency of the subsequent language model. The future research work can be centered on the OCR technology of Guqin jianzi, so as to improve the model performance of the task of transcription. The future research work can be centered on the OCR technology of Guqin jianzi, which can collect a large amount of corpus that can be used for language model training, so as to improve the model performance of the task of transcription.

# References

1. Changlin, C.: Preliminary application of the computer technique to guqin music research. Chin. J. Comput. **07**, 525–533 (1989)
2. Xiaojun, D., Xingting, Y., Changle, Z.: Coding and compilatory method in the transnotation jianzipu of qin zither. Musicol. Chin. **02**, 93–96 (2008)
3. Yang, L., Yingmin, T.: A structured description method of guqin embodied music cognition. J. Beijing Inf. Sci. Technol. Univ. **25**(S2), 61–65 (2010)
4. Dan, H.: Digital application of Guqin Jianzi notation. Printing Field **05**, 59–62 (2014)
5. Qinrong, L.: Discussion on the internet innovation industry model of Chinese traditional music content dissemination-taking guqin digitization as an example. Editors Monthly **05**, 67–71 (2017)
6. Genfang, C.: Overview of digital protection of guqin art and intelligent analysis of temperament. J. Fudan Univ. (Nat. Sci.) **58**(03), 335–342 (2019)
7. Hui, Yu.: The principle of computer automatic processing of pitch information of guqin Jianzi notation. J. Xi'an Conservatory Music **03**, 56–58 (1993)
8. Yali, G.: Guqin Jianzi notation Music' Auto Composition Based on Genetic Algorithm. Xiamen University, Fujian (2009)
9. Songdi, G., Changle, Z.: Translation from modern western score to Guqin Jianzi notation. Mind Comput. **4**(01), 45–54 (2010)
10. Yali, G., Changle, Z.: The creating of guqin corpus and the rule extraction. Mind Comput. **4**(02), 128–138 (2010)
11. Zhuang, X., Zhou, C., Qi, J., Gao, S., Lü, L.: A calculation approach for fetching reduced notation pitch of guqin and its implementation with software. Comput. Appl. Softw. **27**(04), 10–12+37 (2010)
12. Zhang, Y., Liu, H.: An approach of Gu Qin music based on genetic algorithm. Inf. Technol. Inf. (09), 28–30 (2018)
13. Li, S., Wu, Y.: An introduction to a symbolic music dataset of Chinese Guqin pieces and its application example. J. Fudan Univ. Nat. Sci. **59**(03), 276–285 (2020)
14. Wei, B., Wang, Y.: Advanced digitization for ancient Chinese Guqin scores based on mask R-CNN algorithm. In: 2023 IEEE International Conference on Multimedia and Expo Workshops (ICMEW), Brisbane, Australia, 2023, pp. 370–375 (2023). https://doi.org/10.1109/ICMEW59549.2023.00070
15. Huang, C., Duvenaud, D., Gajos, K.Z.: ChordRipple: recommending chords to help novice composers go beyond the ordinary. In: The 21st International Conference, California, USA. New York, USA, pp. 241–250. ACM (2016)
16. Madjiheurem, S., Qu, L., Walder, C. Chord2Vec: learning Musical Chord Embeddings. In: Proceedings of the Constructive Machine Learning Workshop at 30th Conference on Neural Information Processing Systems (NIPS2016), Barcelona, Spain (2016)
17. Herremans, D., Chuan, C.H.: Modeling musical context with Word2vec. In: First International Workshop on Deep Learning and Music, Anchorage, US, pp. 11–18 (2017)
18. Chuan, C.H., Agres, K., Herremans, D.: From context to concept: exploring semantic relationships in music with word2vec. Neural Comput. Appl. **32**, 1023–1036 (2020)
19. Liang, H., Lei, W., Chan, P., et al.: PiRhDy: learning pitch-, rhythm-, and dynamics-aware embeddings for symbolic music. In: Proceedings of the 28th ACM International Conference on Multimedia (MM 2020), Seattle, USA. New York, USA, pp. 574–582. ACM (2020)

20. Hirai, T., Sawada, S.: Melody2Vec: distributed representations of melodic phrases based on melody segmentation. J. Inf. Process. **27**, 278–286 (2019)

21. Tsai, T., Ji ,K.: Composer style classification of piano sheet music images using language model pretraining. In: International Society for Music Information Retrieval Conference, pp. 176–183 (2020)

22. Chou, Y.H., Chen, I.C., Chang, C.J., et al.: MidiBERT-piano: large-scale pre-training for symbolic music understanding. arXiv Preprint. arXiv: 2107.05223

23. Zeng, M., Tan, X., Wang, R., et al.: MusicBERT: symbolic music understanding with large-scale pre-training. In: Findings of the Association for Computational (ACL), Bangkok, Thailand (2021)

24. Wang, Z., Xia, G.: MuseBERT: pre-training music representation for music understanding and controllable generation. In: International Society for Music Information Retrieval, pp. 722–729 (2021)

25. Dongshen, P., Dianying, Z.: Graded Guqin Repertoire 1. People's Music Publishing House, Beijing (2010)

26. Xiangting, L., Yi, G.: Graded Guqin Repertoire 2. People's Music Publishing House, Beijing (2010)

27. Chen, L.: Analysis of fingering signs for Gu Qin. Chinese Music (03), 30–40+168 (2020)

28. Sahrawat, D., et al.: Keyphrase extraction as sequence labeling using contextualized embeddings. In: Jose, J.M., et al. (eds.) ECIR 2020. LNCS, vol. 12036, pp. 328–335. Springer, Cham (2020). https://doi.org/10.1007/978-3-030-45442-5_41

29. Xu, L., Li, S., Wang, Y., Xu, L.: Named entity recognition of BERT-BiLSTM-CRF combined with self-attention. In: Xing, C., Fu, X., Zhang, Y., Zhang, G., Borjigin, C. (eds.) WISA 2021. LNCS, vol. 12999, pp. 556–564. Springer, Cham (2021). https://doi.org/10.1007/978-3-030-87571-8_48

# Music Generation

# Towards the Implementation of an Automatic Composition System for Popular Songs

Di Lu, Qingwen Zhou, and Xiaobing Li[✉]

Central Conservatory of Music, Beijing, China
{ld,zqingwen,lxiaobing}@ccom.edu.cn

**Abstract.** Lyrics are the most recognizable part of a popular song, and corresponding singing voice makes it easy to convey the emotion and experience inside the lyrics to the listeners. However, most current automatic composition systems that can generate pop music lack the consideration for lyrics and singing voice. In this paper, we propose an Integrated architecture of Automatic composition system concerned with Singing voice from given lyrics for popular songs (IAmSinging). With the help of a three-stage pipeline, score, performance and audio files can be generated for users easily. To evaluate the feasibility and availability, we implemented a user-friendly web-based application named CCOM AI-composition system based on this architecture. The experimental results indicates that the system can generate satisfactory results and could be an enjoyable solution for musical amateurs.

**Keywords:** Automatic Composition System · Song Generation · Singing Voice Syntheses

## 1 Introduction

Music has a great influence on our everyday life. Of all the music genres, pop music is the most common type of song in the music industry. With the rapid development of AI, how to generate pop music automatically has become a hot topic in recent years. Many interesting works have been done by worldwide companies and research institutes in this area. Applications that can generate pop music even the users do not have any knowledge of music have emerged. Apple's GarageBand [1] allows users to create music easily through combination with a complete sound library that includes instruments, presets for guitar and voice, and an incredible selection of session drummers and percussionists. Band-in-a-Box [2], DigiBand [3] and Youband [4] can generate multi-track music based on user-specified parameters such as genre, emotion, chord and so on. But these software basically utilize template-based methods and only support rule-based modifications. Aiva [5] is Deep Learning-based and can create music for commercial activity. The generated results are very promising but lyrics input is not supported. Orpheus [6] allows user to input Japanese lyrics and can generate a full song, while iComposer [7] allows user to input Chinese lyrics and can generate a piece of melody. But the quality is not as good as commercial applications.

As shown in Table 1, it is noteworthy that lyrics input, as an important part in a popular song, is not supported in most applications, and consequently there is no singing voice mixed in the generated song. Although Youband [4] and Orpheus [6] supports lyrics input and singing voice synthesis, the quality of generated result cannot reach the level of industrial applications.

In this paper, we will introduce an integrated architecture towards the implementation of an automatic composition system for popular songs concerned with the lyric and singing voice.

**Table 1.** Comparison of different automatic composition systems.

| Automatic Composition systems | Properties | | | | | |
|---|---|---|---|---|---|---|
| | Commercial | DL-based | Multitrack | Lyrics input | Singing voice | Timbre quality |
| GarageBand [1] | √ | | √ | | | √ |
| Band-in-a-Box [2] | √ | | √ | | | √ |
| DigiBand [3] | √ | | √ | | | |
| YouBand [4] | √ | | √ | √ | √ | |
| AIVA [5] | √ | √ | √ | | | √ |
| Orpheus [6] | | | √ | √ | √ | |
| iComposer [7] | | √ | | √ | | |

## 2 Background

It is not difficult for human beings to create popular songs. When there is a need or requirement for a new popular song, for the first step, one or more composers will start to produce a music score, which includes melody, lyrics and accompaniment. Then, the performers need to convert the notes in the score into physical actions with precise control on the instrument. Through their control of performance elements, the performers can make the song more expressive and characteristic. With the help of the performers, the singing voice by the singer and the sound by the instruments can be recoded and mixed as an audio file, such as MP3 and WAV. Finally, the sound can be perceived directly by the listener.

As shown in Fig. 1, the music generation process is usually divided into three stages [8]: score generation, performance generation and sound generation. Similarly, automatic popular song generation can also be divided into these stages [9]: score generation, performance generation and audio generation. Each stage is conditioned on the results of previous stages, which means performance is predicted by score features, and audio is generated based on score and performance.

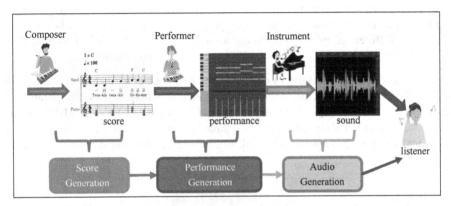

**Fig. 1.** Process of music generation.

## 3 System Overview

The ultimate goal of an automatic composition system is to allow the users, regardless of their musical knowledge or background, to create a song as required automatically. Generally, the users would like to input some parameters by an interface to tell the system what kind of song they want, and hope the system can output a desired song in audio format such as MP3 or WAV. Some professional users may also want MIDI format that contains all the information of generated score. Moreover, the output song should contain not only the well-performed instrumental sounds, but also a good-sounding singing voice.

Here are some parameters that are widely used in the applications mentioned at the beginning of this paper. Some parameters are very straightforward for music amateurs, while others are difficult and more suitable for music professionals.

- Genre: Popular songs often contains elements of other music genres. This parameter refers to the subgenres under the umbrella of pop music, which may include folk, electronic, R&B, rock, hip-hop and so on.
- Emotion: This parameter indicates what kind of emotion the users want to express by the song. For example, cheerful, sad, excited, peaceful and so on.
- Structure: This parameter refers to how a song is organized, using a combination of different sections. A typical song structure includes verse, chorus, and bridge. For example, a common song may be organized in Verse-Verse-Chorus-Chorus form.

- Tempo: This parameter indicates the speed of the song. Usually it can be called BPM (Beat Per Minute) that represents the number of beats played in one minute. The value 50 means the song is very slow, while 160 means the song is very fast.
- Tonality: This parameter includes key note and scale of the song.
- Instrument: This parameter allows users to choose the instruments they want to arrange in generated accompaniment. For example, if the user only chooses a piano, the generated accompaniment will be a piano solo.
- Chord progression: Chord is a harmonic collection of two or more notes with different pitches playing at the same time. Chord progression is a sequence of chords when multiple different chords are played one after the other. For example, I-V-vi-iii-IV-I-IV-V is a typical chord progression that can be used in pop music.

Figure 2 shows the overview of our proposed automatic composition system. In the system, the generation process is realized as a pipeline, whose input is the parameters mentioned above and output is the file in audio format (MP3, WAV) or MIDI format. According to Sect. 2, the pipeline consists of three modules: score generator, performance generator and audio generator, which will be discussed in the next section.

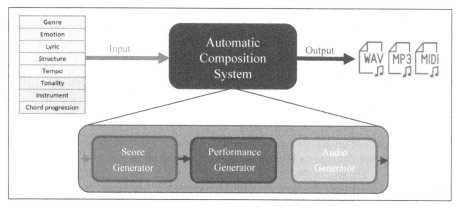

**Fig. 2.** Overview of our proposed automatic composition system.

# 4 Generator Modules

In this section, we will provide methodologies which are necessary for song generation. Details of each generator module will be introduced respectively.

## 4.1 Score Generator

The major goal of score generator is to output a score based on input parameters, which is composed of vocal melody and accompaniment. In score generator, at first, the parameters will be sent into a Parameter Preprocessor to ensure the input is correct. If any parameter is not inputted, it will be chosen or generated automatically. After preprocessing, all the information in the score is specified except for melody and accompaniment. Then, the vocal melody will be generated by Melody Generator based on the parameters. And the accompaniment will be generated by Accompaniment Generator based on the parameters and vocal melody. At last, the vocal melody and accompaniment will be integrated as a full score. The whole process is shown in Fig. 3.

**Melody Generator.** As the main task of melody generator, generating melody from lyrics can be regarded as the task of song writing or lyrics-to-melody generation. There have been some non-deep learning researches [10–12] and neuron-based methods [7, 13–16] on this task. We also did some related works [17, 18] using transformer-based model. Although these models could produce some good pieces, but some of pieces are poor musicality and the attention learned is messed and of poor structure, which is fatal for industrial use. Therefore, we introduced a rule-guided refiner model to refine generated music pieces with high musicality.

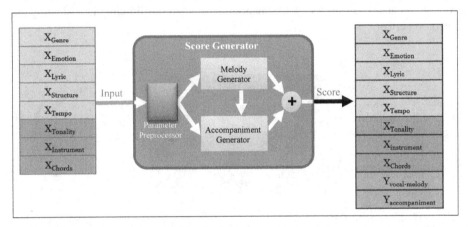

**Fig. 3.** Score generator.

**Accompaniment Generator.** Generating accompaniment can be regarded as the task of multi-track or multi-instrument generation. In most commercial applications, a pattern databank is prepared beforehand with large amount of music clips, templates or loops in it. While generating accompaniment, patterns are extracted from the databank by certain rules and then combined together as a full accompaniment. There are also some researches based-on deep learning [13, 19–21]. However, due to the lack of well-labelled accompaniment dataset, this kind of models can only generate accompaniment of limited styles and instruments. The generation effect is not promising and still far from the traditional method. As a result, traditional methods are highly recommended to use for accompaniment generation especially for commercial purpose.

## 4.2  Performance Generator

After the score of vocal melody and accompaniment are generated, the score will be sent to performance generator to make the score more expressive. Through this module, music expressions, such as tempo change, dynamics, velocity, and timing information will be added to the score. At last, all the performance will be integrated together as output. The whole process is shown in Fig. 4.

There are two submodules for singer performance generation and instrument performance generation respectively, because singer performance and instrument performance may be affected by different features.

Similar to the algorithms of score generation, performance generation methods also include rule-based method, probability model and deep learning. Rule-based stochastic model [22–24] is widely used in most applications. There are also some researches based-on Deep Learning [25–32]. With the help of performance datasets, which contains performance data and corresponding music score, neural network can be trained for this task. But different with score generation, there are not much research on this task, probably because of the lack of performance datasets and the difficulty in evaluating the generation effect.

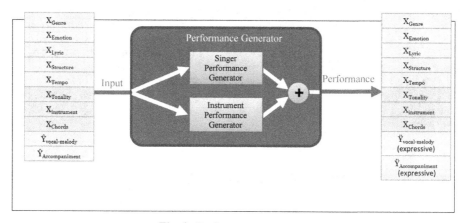

**Fig. 4.** Performance generator.

Actually, performance generator can be emitted in this system, because the whole pipeline can still work without this module. In our practice, we regard performance generation as a subtask of score generation or a subtask of audio generation. Specifically, instrument performance is usually well prepared when building accompaniment data-bank, while singer performance can be generated during the process of singing voice synthesis, which will be introduced in the following section.

## 4.3  Audio Generator

Audio generation is to generate audio files directly from the score of vocal melody and accompaniment with expressive performance. There are two submodules for singing voice synthesis and instrumental sound synthesis respectively, because singing voice and instrumental sound have different features while training the model. At last, singing voice and instrumental sound will be mixed together as output. The whole process is shown in Fig. 5.

The algorithm of instrumental sound synthesis and singing voice synthesis are very similar to the algorithm of Text-to-speech. For instrumental sound synthesis, almost all the DAWs (Digital Audio Workstation) are using Concatenative Synthesis in the industrial field. For researchers, A DAW named Reaper [33] is recommended since it's programmable via python or Lua script. With the help of numerous audio plugins, studio-quality instrumental sound can be produced.

For singing voice, previous successful singing-voice synthesizers are based on concatenative methods [34, 35]. But in recent years, deep learning [36–40] is more effective than traditional methods both in sound quality and naturalness. In out practice, we use HiFiSinger [40] as acoustic model and HiFi-GAN [41] as a vocoder for singing voice synthesis. Both models are slightly modified to improve the quality and naturalness of generated singing voice.

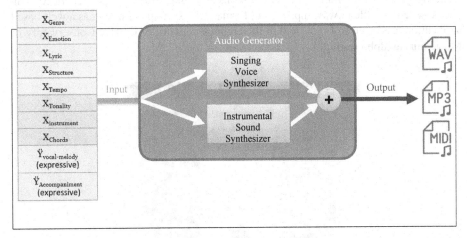

**Fig. 5.**  Audio generator.

## 4.4  Pipeline

The automatic composition pipeline is composed of three generator modules and shown in this Fig. 6. After the users input the parameters, the system can generate score, performance and audio files for the users.

It should be noted that, not all the submodules are necessarily implemented with deep learning method. Some traditional methods are still state-of-the-art solutions.

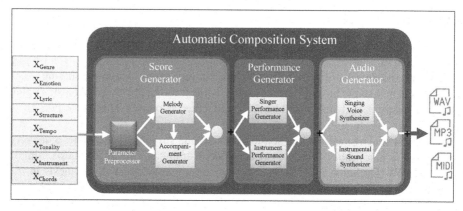

**Fig. 6.** Pipeline of IAmSinging.

## 5 Implementation

CCOM AI-composition system is an automatic composition system for Chinese popular songs that we implemented based on the architecture described in above sections. It's very easy to use for both musical amateurs and professionals. The whole song is computed from the lyrics input with choices of emotions and song structure, and generated song can be saved as a file in.wav,.mp3 or.mid format. The system is running as a web-based application as shown in Fig. 7 within the campus network of Central Conservatory of Music during alpha testing.

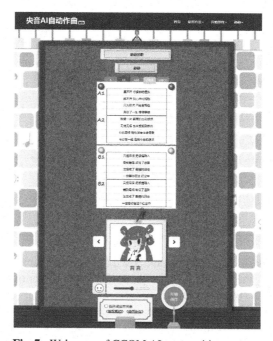

**Fig. 7.** Web page of CCOM AI-composition system.

Three datasets are used for generator modules. CCOM-Comprehensive Analysis of Popular Music Dataset, which contains more than 800 pop songs with features of tempo, tonality, chord progression, structure, note and lyric are well labeled, is used for training transformer-based score generator. We also used CCOM-Popular Singing Voice Dataset for training 3 virtual singers in singing voice synthesizer and CCOM–MIDI for Popular Music Dataset for accompaniment generator. A number of VSTi and VST plugins are used for audio rendering and mixing.

## 6 Experiment

To evaluate the system, we did two subjective experiments. Firstly, we asked 20 musical professionals to evaluate 10 randomly generated songs in five-grade evaluation. Secondly, we ask 20 musical amateurs and 20 musical professionals to use our system and answer the questions about the system and the generated songs by scoring from '1' for bad to '5' for good.

The results of the first experiment are shown in Fig. 8, which demonstrates that more than three-quarters of generated songs can follow music theory strictly, and the attractiveness of more than 68.5% of generated songs is above average.

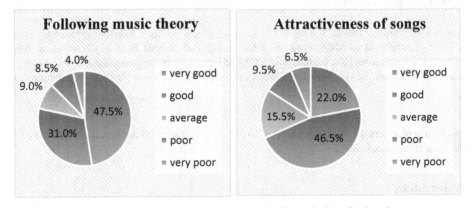

**Fig. 8.** Evaluation results on 10 songs by 20 musical professionals.

Table 2 shows the results of the second experiment. It can be found that musical ama-teurs gave higher score than musical professionals, probably because it's a pleasant surprise for them that a pop song could be created in spite of their little experience with composition and music theory.

The experimental results enable us to conclude that the system can generate promising result that follows music theory and is able to generate good songs in some cases. Unexpectedly, we found that our system is an enjoyable solution for musical amateurs. Furthermore, the implementation of the system proved the feasibility and availability of our proposed architecture IAmSinging.

**Table 2.** Evaluation results on the system by 20 musical amateurs and 20 musical professionals.

|  | Musical amateurs | Musical professionals |
|---|---|---|
| Are generated songs satisfactory? | 3.60 | 3.55 |
| Had fun when trying this system? | 4.05 | 3.45 |

## 7   Conclusion and Future Works

This research attempted to design an automatic composition system for popular song generation with lyrics and singing voice, which enables users to create their original songs easily.

However, there might be a need for larger data scale. In our tasks, popular song dataset and singing voice dataset are needed for training corresponding models. We have been trying to create our own datasets for years, but the data is still far from enough. It's important for us to keep increasing the amount of data, as well as the quality and richness of data.

Moreover, our system can only generate songs up to 90 s long, but the typical song length is 3–4 min. Consequently, we expect more studies to be carried out in improving capacity of generating longer song.

**Acknowledgments.** Thanks for the anonymous reviewers for their valuable comments. This research is supported by Major Projects of National Social Science Fund of China (Grant No. 21ZD19). We also would like to thank all CCOM AI lab members for useful discussions on topics related to this work, and conservatory students involved in this project for their contributions to dataset.

**Disclosure of Interests.** The authors have no competing interests to declare that are relevant to the content of this article.

## References

1. GarageBand Homepage. https://www.apple.com/mac/garageband/. Accessed 18 Nov 2023
2. Band-in-a-Box Homepage. https://www.bandinabox.com/. Accessed 18 Nov 2023
3. DigiBand Homepage. https://www.athtek.com/digiband.html. Accessed 18 Nov 2023
4. YouBand Homepage. http://dsoundsoft.com/product/youband/. Accessed 18 Nov 2023
5. AIVA Homepage. https://aiva.ai/. Accessed 18 Nov 2023
6. Orpheus Homepage. https://www.orpheus-music.org/. Accessed 18 Nov 2023
7. Lee, H.-P., Fang, J.-S., Ma, W.-Y.: iComposer: An automatic song writing system for Chinese popular music. In: Proceedings of the 2019 Conference of the North American Chapter of the Association for Computational Linguistics (Demonstrations), pp. 84–88 (2019)
8. Oore, S., Simon, I., Dieleman, S., Eck, D., Simonyan, K.: This time with feeling: learning expressive musical performance. Neural Comput. Appl. **32**(4), 955–967 (2020)
9. Ji, S., Luo, J., Yang, X.: A comprehensive survey on deep music generation multi-level representations, algorithms, evaluations, and future directions. arXiv preprint: arXiv:2011. 06801 (2020)

10. Fukayama, S., et al.: Orpheus: automatic composition system considering prosody of Japanese lyrics. In: Natkin, S., Dupire, J. (eds.) Entertainment Computing – ICEC 2009. Lecture Notes in Computer Science, vol. 5709, pp. 309–310. Springer, Berlin (2009). https://doi.org/10.1007/978-3-642-04052-8_47

11. Scirea, M., Barros, G.A., Shaker, N., Togelius, J.: Smug: Scientific music generator. In: Proceedings of the Sixth International Conference on Computational Creativity June, pp. 204 (2015)

12. Ackerman, M., Loker, D.: Algorithmic songwriting with ALYSIA. In: Correia, J., Ciesielski, V., Liapis, A. (eds.) Computational Intelligence in Music, Sound, Art and Design. Evo-MUSART 2017. Lecture Notes in Computer Science(), vol. 10198, pp. 1–16. Springer, Cham (2017). https://doi.org/10.1007/978-3-319-55750-2_1

13. Zhu, H., et al: Xiaoice band: a melody and arrangement generation framework for pop music. In: Proceedings of the 24th ACM SIGKDD International Conference on Knowledge Discovery & Data Mining, pp. 2837–2846 (2018)

14. Bao, H. et al.: Neural melody composition from lyrics. In: Tang, J., Kan, MY., Zhao, D., Li, S., Zan, H. (eds.) Natural Language Processing and Chinese Computing. NLPCC 2019. Lecture Notes in Computer Science(), vol. 11838, pp. 499–511. Springer, Cham (2018). https://doi.org/10.1007/978-3-030-32233-5_39

15. Yu, Y., Harscoët, F., Canales, S., Reddy M,G., Tang, S., Jiang, J.: Lyrics-conditioned neural melody generation. In: Ro, Y., et al. (eds.) MultiMedia Modeling. MMM 2020. Lecture Notes in Computer Science(), vol. 11962, pp. 709–714. Springer, Cham (2020)

16. Ju, Z., et al.: TeleMelody: lyric-to-melody generation with a template-based two-stage method. arXiv preprint: arXiv:2109.09617 (2021)

17. Wang, W., Li, X., Jin, C., Lu, D., Zhou, Q., Tie, Y.: CPS: full-song and style-conditioned music generation with linear transformer. In: 2022 IEEE International Conference on Multimedia and Expo Workshops (ICMEW), pp. 18–22 (2022)

18. Liu, J., et al.: Symphony generation with permutation invariant language model. In: International Society for Music Information Retrieval (ISMIR) (2022)

19. Chu, H., Urtasun, R., Fidler, S.: Song from PI: a musically plausible network for pop music generation. In: International Conference on Learning Representations (ICLR), Workshop Track (2016)

20. Dong, H.W., Hsiao, W.Y., Yang, L.C., Yang, Y.H.: MuseGAN: multi-track sequential generative adversarial networks for symbolic music generation and accompaniment. In: AAAI, pp. 34–41 (2018)

21. Ren, Y., He, J., Tan, X., Qin, T., Zhao, Z., Liu, T.Y.: PopMAG: Pop music accompaniment generation. In: Proceedings of the 28th ACM International Conference on Multimedia, pp. 1198–1206 (2020)

22. Friberg, A.: PDM: an expressive sequencer with real-time control of the kth music-performance rules. Comput. Music. J. **30**(1), 37–48 (2006)

23. Grindlay, G., Helmbold, D.: Modeling, analyzing, and synthesizing expressive piano performance with graphical models. Mach. Learn. **65**(2–3), 361–387 (2006)

24. Flossmann, S., Grachten, M., Widmer, G.: Expressive performance rendering with probabilistic models. In: Kirke, A., Miranda, E. (eds.) Guide to Computing for Expressive Music Performance, pp. 75–98. Springer, London (2013). https://doi.org/10.1007/978-1-4471-4123-5_3

25. Cancino-Chacón, C.E., Gadermaier, T., Widmer, G., Grachten, M.: An evaluation of linear and non-linear models of expressive dynamics in classical piano and symphonic music. Mach. Learn. **106**(6), 887–909 (2017)

26. Jeong, D., Kwon, T., Kim, Y., Lee, K., Nam, J.: VirtuosoNet: a hierarchical RNN-based system for modeling expressive piano performance. In: ISMIR, pp. 908–915 (2019)

27. Simon, I., Oore, S.: Performance RNN: generating music with expressive timing and dynamics. Magenta Blog:https://magenta.tensorflow.org/performance-rnn (2017)

28. Maezawa, A.: Deep piano performance rendering with conditional VAE. In: 19th International Society for Music Information Retrieval Conference (ISMIR) Late Breaking and Demo Papers (2018)

29. Jeong, D., Kwon, T., Kim, Y., Nam, J.,: Graph neural network for music score data and modeling expressive piano performance. In: International Conference on Machine Learning, pp. 3060–3070 (2019)

30. Hawthorne, C., Huang, A., Ippolito, D., Eck, D.: Transformer-nade for piano performances. In: submission, NIPS Second Workshop on Machine Learning for Creativity and Design (2018)

31. Choi, K., Hawthorne, C., Simon, I., Dinculescu, M., Engel, J.: Encoding musical style with transformer autoencoders. arXiv preprint: arXiv:1912.05537 (2019)

32. Huang, Y.-S., Yang, Y.-H.: Pop music transformer: Beat-based modeling and generation of expressive pop piano compositions. In: Proceedings of the 28th ACM International Conference on Multimedia, pp. 1180–1188 (2020)

33. Reaper Homepage. https://www.reaper.fm/. Accessed 18 Nov 2023

34. Bonada, J., Umbert Morist, M., Blaauw, M.: Expressive singing synthesis based on unit selection for the singing synthesis challenge 2016. In: Proceedings Interspeech 2016, pp. 1230-1234 (2016)

35. Bonada, J., Serra, X.: Synthesis of the singing voice by performance sampling and spectral models. IEEE Signal Process. Mag. **24**(2), 67–79 (2007)

36. Hono, Y., et al.: Recent development of the DNN-based singing voice synthesis system—sinsy. In: 2018 Asia-Pacific Signal and Information Processing Association Annual Summit and Conference (APSIPA ASC), pp. 1003–1009 (2018)

37. Kim, J., Choi, H., Park, J., Kim, S., Kim, J., Hahn, M.: Korean singing voice synthesis system based on an LSTM recurrent neural network. In: INTERSPEECH, pp. 1551–1555 (2018)

38. Lu, P., Wu, J., Luan, J., Tan, X., Zhou, L.: XiaoiceSing: a high-quality and integrated singing voice synthesis system. Proceedings Interspeech 2020, pp. 1306-1310 (2020)

39. Gu, Y., et al: A chinese singing voice synthesis system using duration allocated encoder-decoder acoustic models and waveRNN vocoders. In: 2021 12th International Symposium on Chinese Spoken Language Processing (ISCSLP), pp. 1–5 (2021)

40. Chen, J., Tan, X., Luan, J., Qin, T., Liu, T.Y.: HiFiSinger: towards high-fidelity neural singing voice synthesis. arXiv preprint: arXiv:2009.01776 (2020)

41. Kong, J., Kim, J., Bae, J.: HiFi-GAN: generative adversarial networks for efficient and high fidelity speech synthesis. In: Proceedings of the 34th International Conference on Neural Information Processing Systems (NIPS'20). Curran Associates Inc., Red Hook, NY, USA, pp. 17022–17033 (2020). Article 1428

# CoCoFormer: A Controllable Feature-Rich Polyphonic Music Generation Method

Jiuyang Zhou⬤, Tengfei Niu⬤, Hong Zhu(✉), and Xingping Wang

Xi'an University of Technology, Xi'an 710048, China
{2210320121,2220321230}@stu.xaut.edu.cn, {zhuhong,
wangxingping}@xaut.edu.cn

**Abstract.** This paper explores the modeling method of polyphonic music sequence. Due to the great potential of Transformer models in music generation, controllable music generation is receiving more attention. In the task of polyphonic music, current controllable generation research focuses on controlling the generation of chords but lacks precise adjustment for the controllable generation of choral music textures. This paper proposes a Condition Choir Transformer (CoCoFormer) which controls the model's output by controlling the input of the chord and rhythm at a fine-grained level. This paper's self-supervised method improves the loss function and performs joint training through conditional control input and unconditional input training. This paper adds an adversarial training method to alleviate the lack of diversity in generated samples caused by teacher-forcing training. CoCoFormer enhances model performance with explicit and implicit inputs to chords and rhythms. In this paper, the experiments show that CoCoFormer has reached much better performance when compared to existing approaches. Based on specifying the polyphonic music texture, the same melody can also be generated in various ways.

**Keywords:** Music language model · polyphonic music generation · symbolic music generation · relative positional attention · controllable generation

## 1 Introduction

Music can be seen as an ordered combination of notes. According to music theory, notes are combined into parts, and multi-part notes constitute a rich musical texture. The temporal and spatial characteristics contained in a piece of music are defined as the textures of the music. According to different textures, music is divided into monophonic music, homophonic and polyphonic. Monophonic music contains only one melody line, which is the form of ancient music and most folk songs. Homophonic has a prominent melody line; other parts are subordinate to the main melody, such as harmony and accompaniment. Polyphonic music consists of several independent melodies. The lines are combined to reflect the characteristics of polyphonic music through different harmonies and polyphonic techniques. From the perspective of texture, the texture of monophonic music contains melody, the texture of homophonic music has horizontal melody and vertical harmony, and the texture of polyphonic music includes two forms of polyphony and harmony, as shown in Fig. 1.

Computer modeling of polyphonic music has been studied for decades, starting in the 1960s [1]. In recent years, much of the progress in music generative models has been due to the continued development and application of neural networks. Models in natural language processing have been widely used in music generation. Sequence modeling has always been the standard choice for music modeling, from early hidden Markov models to RNN [2], LSTM [3], BiLSTM [4], and other RNN methods; in addition to sequence modeling, a piece of music can be converted into a piano roll, and images can also be input. CNN trained as a generative adversarial network for music generation [5]. Some recent work revolves around Transformer [6]. Music Transformer [7] proposes a new relative attention mechanism and reduces the complexity of the model to linear as the sequence increases. MuseNet [8] uses a Transformer model based on GPT-2 [9], which has been used in an amount of Music training can generate various styles of music such as classical and jazz.

The texture of polyphonic music can be seen as a combination of horizontal melodic features and vertical chord features. Chord features can be used as additional input to improve the generation quality of music models. The input in [10] has pitch and chord information, uses the expert system of the LSTM model [11] to generate jazz, MidiNet [12] uses CNN combined with GAN to generate music, and adds chord sequences for auxiliary prediction. But none of these methods can predict chords as input for each step, but treat them as fixed input.

**Fig. 1.** The embodiment of texture in polyphonic music: the horizontal melody structure and the vertical harmony structure constitute the texture, which is embodied in specific rhythm and pitch. The left and right pictures use the same main melody, but the texture characteristics are entirely different, and people's hearing is also different.

The research on the harmony of polyphonic music has always taken the choral hymn data set of Johann Sebastian Bach as the research object [13, 14], and the research goal is to generate polyphonic music that is like Bach as possible. For example, BachBot [15] uses the LSTM structure to generate choral music, DeepBach [16] uses Deep-RNN for feature extraction and has been used in Monteverdi's five-part madrigal and Palestrina's mass. TonicNet [17] uses chord and pitch information and the number of repetitions of notes as data input, using GRU [18] for feature extraction. DeepChoir used the stacking structure of BiLSTM for sequence modeling and used the harmony consistency evaluation method of chords and melody to evaluate the results to generate chorus musicality.

Polyphonic music has two expression techniques: polyphony and harmony, embodying harmony and rhythm. The chords and rhythm of the melody reflect the textural characteristics of polyphonic music. This paper starts from the perspective of controllable music generation of polyphonic music textures, uses a self-attention mechanism to build a polyphonic music generation model CoCoFormer (Condition-Choir-Transformer), and selects Bach's choral hymns as a training sample set. This paper proposes a way to combine additional information explicitly and implicitly into the model and proposes a self-supervised learning method to construct a loss function for better training. Experiments have proven that CoCoFormer has achieved the best performance of known polyphonic music generation models.

The contributions of this paper are:

1. This paper propose a polyphonic music generation model CoCoFormer based on texture features, which can generate controllable choral music and proves the effectiveness of each module.
2. Introduce a self-supervised learning method, using multiple loss functions for joint training.
3. Through experiments, this paper studies how CoCoFormer controls music generation by controlling texture characteristics and generates music samples with precise control.

## 2 Related Work

Recursive neural networks have potent capabilities for modeling sequence data. RNN-based models [19] have been widely used in music generation. The earliest example is to use RNN [20, 21] to simulate single-note music. LSTM and other methods alleviate long-term dependence based on RNN models, replacing RNN as a more effective method.

In recent models, DeepBach adds extensions and beat marks while inputting pitch information. Through the forward DeepRNN [22] and reverse DeepRNN, the two modules perform bidirectional sequential extraction of features and output the probability of pitch. They are using pseudo-Gibbs sampling to simulate the process of artificial composition. The input of the TonicNet model includes word embeddings of chord and pitch information and word embeddings of input note repetition times, which are spliced and then input into the encoder. However, in generating long sequences, global and local information cannot be combined, and it is hard to learn the relationship between long-distance notes. The DeepChoir [23] model is a multi-head autoregressive encoding and decoding structure model. It uses the melody, chord information, rhythm, extension marks, and the notes of the soprano part as input and is encoded through a three-layer Bi-LSTM [24]. The output layer uses gamma sampling output.

In general, RNN-based models make the generated music more musical, and the additional information also improves the performance in generating polyphonic music. However, as the generated sequence continues to grow in application, it is difficult for the model to consider both global and local information to generate accurate notes.

Experiments show that the self-attention mechanism is significantly better than RNN-based models in establishing long-range dependencies [25], and its ability to extract semantic features is also higher than RNN-based models, indicating that Transformer is more suitable for music generation than RNN structures. For example, MusicTransformer adds relative position attention based on the structure of the Transformer and optimizes the time complexity of establishing long sequences. LakhNES [26] uses the structure of TransformerXL [27], is trained on a large four-part music library, and is evaluated on the NES dataset [28]. MuseNet is based on the GPT2 [29] model and trained on many music data sets to predict the next token through unsupervised learning. In the direction of polyphonic music generation, Transformer models are rarely used in polyphonic music generation, and they also need more controllability of polyphonic music textures.

This paper proposes the CoCoFormer model. Because of the controllable problem of the current model in generating music, a polyphonic music generation method based on controllable chords and rhythm is proposed. Because of the auxiliary additional information, this paper designed a new structure to input a combination of chords and rhythms with a specific structure to extract the feature vectors of chords and rhythms and fuse them with the attention matrix to combine the vectors of polyphonic music explicitly and implicitly. This method enhances the controllability of the model texture.

# 3   Proposed Model CoCoFormer

Give a prompt message $x_{con} = \{c_1, \ldots, c_n\}$ and note sequence $x = \{x_1, x_2, \ldots, x_T\}$, joint probability $P(x|x_{con}) = \prod_t P(x_t|x_{<t}, x_{con})$. The task of this paper is to generate a model through an autoregression model, learn the factorization formula of $P(x|x_{con})$ distribution through an autoregressive generative model, encode the polyphonic music into a fixed-size feature matrix, and decode it through softmax to get the output of the next token.

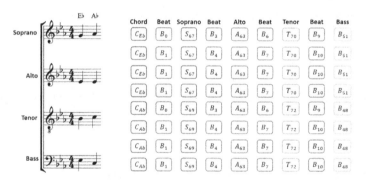

**Fig. 2.** Data representation of notes is arranged in sixteenth note resolution.

This paper will introduce CoCoFormer through data representation, model structure, and loss function construction.

## 3.1   Data Representation

In symbolic music generation, the pitch, chord, rhythm, and other information of each note are represented by specific events. This paper first defines the representation of events. Referring to the midi coding and defining 128 pitch events. For chord events, 49 types of events given in the data set are used, including 12 types of major chords, minor chords, augmented chords, diminished chords, and a category of other chords. Rhythm events give three states of notes under different voices: note start, rest, and note hold, a total of 12 types of events.

Given a symbol sequence of four parts of polyphonic music, and define the relevant markers: note marks: note $= \{N_s^0, N_a^0, N_t^0, N_b^0, \ldots, N_s^n, N_a^n, N_t^n, N_b^n\}$, chord marks: chord $= \{C^0, C^1, C^2, \ldots, C^n\}$, rhythm marks: beat $= \{B_s^0, B_a^0, B_t^0, B_b^0, \ldots, B_s^n, B_a^n, B_t^n, B_b^n\}$, as shown in Fig. 2.

The data input is expressed as:

$$\text{Condition input}_{chord} = \left\{ C^0, C^1, C^2, \ldots, C^n \right\} \tag{1}$$

$$\text{Condition input}_{beat} = \left\{ B_s^0, B_a^0, B_t^0, B_b^0, \ldots, B_s^n, B_a^n, B_t^n, B_b^n \right\} \tag{2}$$

$$\text{Input} = \left\{ C^0, B_s^0, N_s^0, B_a^0, N_a^0, B_t^0, N_t^0, B_b^0, N_b^0, \ldots, C^n, B_s^n, N_s^n, B_a^n, N_a^n, B_t^n, N_t^n, B_b^n, N_b^n \right\} \tag{3}$$

The superscript of the mark is time, the sequence length is n, and the subscripts of rhythm mark and pitch mark represent different parts, s, a, t and b, respectively representing female high, female low, male high, and male low. Department, superscript indicates time.

## 3.2 CoCoFormer

This paper starts from the perspective of controllable texture and proposes the CoCo-Former model through explicit and implicit input of chords and rhythms. As shown in Fig. 3, in the first stage, two single-layer standard Transformer encoders containing attention layers and feed-forward layers are designed to learn implicit expressions of rhythm and chords and concatenate them into the Transformer in stage two. The features are concatenated with the attention layer of the first Transformer layer. After the subsequent Transformer layers in the second stage, an attention layer that adds relative positions is used to learn the relationship between notes. The features are decoded to generate polyphonic music.

From Eqs. (1) and (2), through token embedding and position embedding, the input chord and rhythm sequences are obtained $x_{chord} \in R^{l_c \times d_p}$, $x_{beat} \in R^{l_b \times d_p}$, where $d_{(\cdot)}$, $l_c$, $l_b$ respectively represent the feature dimension, the length of the chord sequence, and the length of the rhythm sequence. $H_{chord} \in R^{l_c \times d_p}$, $h_{beat} \in R^{l_b \times d_p}$ are obtained through two Transformers $\text{Model}_{chord}$, $\text{Model}_{beat}$ with the same structure but different sizes, such as (4) (5):

$$H_{chord} = \text{Model}_{chord}(x_{chord}) \tag{4}$$

$$H_{beat} = \text{Model}_{beat}(x_{beat}) \tag{5}$$

After $h_{chord}$, $h_{beat}$ passes through the linear layer, the matrix size is calculated unchanged with the corresponding $K_{chord}$, $V_{chord}$, $K_{beat}$, and $V_{beat}$. Then, concatenate

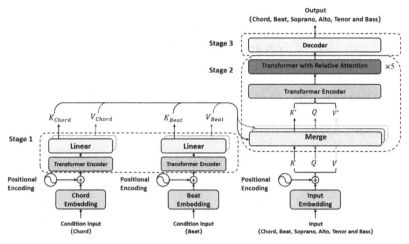

**Fig. 3.** The structure of CoCoFormer is divided into three parts: conditional input in Stage 1, feature extraction in Stage 2, and decoding in Stage 3

features with input, such as (6), and calculate the attention and feed-forward layers as (7):

$$K' = [K_{chord}, K_{beat}, K], V' = [V_{chord}, V_{beat}, V] \tag{6}$$

$$A = \text{Softmax}\left(QK'^T\right)V', h_{out1} = \text{FFN}(A) \tag{7}$$

The backbone Transformer in the second stage is used to process polyphonic music features that add chords and rhythms. It is composed of the Decoder with attention adding relative position relationships, such as Eq. (8), where $R_I$ represents the relative position relationship.

$$\text{Head}_i = \text{RA}(Q_I, K_I, V_I, R_i) = \text{Softmax}\left(Q_i K_i^T + Q_i R_i\right)V_I \tag{8}$$

$$\text{Multi} - \text{RA}(Q, K, V) = \text{Concat}(\text{head}_1, \dots, \text{head}_n)W^o \tag{9}$$

In the third stage, the Decoder is constructed from three linear layers with normalization and dropout. The features are processed by the linear layer, and the probability of the next token is generated through softmax output:

$$P_t = \text{Softmax}\left(h_{out3(<t)}\right) \tag{10}$$

### 3.3 Loss Function

We train CoCoFormer through a self-supervised method, as shown in Fig. 4. The model input is divided into conditional input and primary input. Naturally, this paper uses different inputs to construct loss functions.

First, use the self-reconstruction method for training. Establish the joint probability $P(x_t) = \prod_t P(x_t|x_{<t}, c = x_{c<t}, x_{b<t})$ of input sequence $x = \{x_1, x_2, \ldots, x_T\}$. X is the conditional input of the model. Under the premise of given conditional input $x_{con}$, , learn the distribution of the sequence, and the loss function constructed is as (11):

$$L_{self} = -\sum_{i=1}^{l} p_i \log_2\left(q_i(x_i|c = x_c, x_b)\right) \tag{11}$$

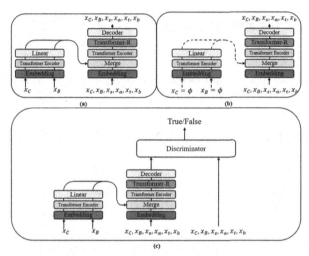

**Fig. 4.** CoCoFormer training method. (a) represents the training process of constructing a self-loss function, using conditional input and primary input for generation training. (b) represents generation training when the conditional input is blank. (c) constructs a discriminator to judge the music generated by the model.

To enable CoCoFormer to generate music smoothly without relying on conditional input, this paper uses a loss function similar to (10), but only uses input, set $input_{chord} = \varnothing$ and $input_{beat} = \varnothing$, as (12):

$$L_{null} = -\sum_{i=1}^{l} p_i \log_2(q_i(x_i)) \tag{12}$$

The transformer is trained in a teacher-forced manner, which speeds up the convergence of the model. However, it is subject to ground-truth constraints. It is hoped that the results will correspond to the samples one-to-one, but on the other hand, it also reduces the possibility of generating diversity [30].

Adversarial training objectives have been shown to help generate sample output [31]. Based on this, this paper uses an adversarial training [32] loss function to minimize the loss to facilitate matching the output to the training samples:

$$L_{adv} = -E_x[\log f_{disc}(x)] + E_y[\log(1 - f_{disc}(y))] \tag{13}$$

$f_{disc}$ is a discriminator network consisting of a single layer of Transformer. They are used to determine whether the sample is a sample generated by the model. During the back-propagation process, the parameters of CoCoFormer $f_{disc}$ are updated, and the training goal is to minimize the loss function. Parameterize $f_{disc}$ with $\varphi$, then the optimization objective is:

$$\Phi^* = \mathrm{argmin}_{\varphi} L_{\mathrm{adv}} \tag{14}$$

The entire training process is trained through the linear combination of Eqs. (11) (12) (13). CoCoFormer uses the Adam optimizer to optimize the following total loss function:

$$L = \mathrm{argmin}_{\theta} \left( \lambda_{\mathrm{self}} L_{self} + \lambda_{\mathrm{null}} L_{null} + \lambda_{adv} L_{adv} \right) \tag{15}$$

**Table 1.** CoCoFormer ablation experimental results, using verification set accuracy as a metrics

| Component | Choice | | | | | |
|---|---|---|---|---|---|---|
| Baseline | √ | √ | √ | √ | √ | √ |
| Chord cond | | √ | √ | √ | √ | √ |
| Relative attn | | | √ | √ | √ | √ |
| Rhythm cond | | | | √ | √ | √ |
| Loss1 | √ | √ | √ | √ | √ | √ |
| Loss2 | | | | | √ | √ |
| Loss3 | | | | | | √ |
| Accuracy | 0.8615 | 0.8726 | 0.913 | 0.932 | 0.9352 | 0.9404 |

## 4 Experiment

### 4.1 Dataset

This paper selects the JS Fake Chorales data set [14], selected from Bach's hymns with expanding similar music, and manually annotates chord information. The data set contains 500 four-part polyphonic music, with 49 events in the chord part, including 12 major chords, minor chords, augmented chords, diminished chords, and other chords. Note resolution is 16th note. To study the performance of the model on the original data set, this paper did not design any data enhancement method.

### 4.2 Experimental Setup

In the experiments, in the first stage, the Transformer used to process chords and rhythms which is a single layer, the input lengths are 256 and 1024 respectively, attention heads are 8, the dimension of the middle layer of the feedforward layer is 256. Attention matrix in stage two is masked, and the Transformer layer in stage one is not masked. The input length of the Transformer in the second stage is 2048, the attention heads are

8, the dimension of the middle layer of feedforward is 1024, and the dropout is 0.1. The discriminator consists of a linear layer and a single layer of Transformer with 4 attention heads, the dimension of the middle layer of feedforward is 512, and the dropout is 0.5. The model training uses a GTX 1080Ti, and the training time is about 5 h.

## 4.3 Ablation Test

This paper conducts ablation experiments on CoCoFormer and experiments on the structures added to the model and different data representation methods. This paper uses the highest accuracy of the validation set as a metric. As shown in Table 1, baseline represents the Transformer baseline, and Chord cond describes adding conditional chord information and the corresponding network. Relative attn represents using relative positional attention in the second stage. Rhythm cond means adding conditional rhythm information and the related processing network. The loss functions Loss1 and Loss2 use the cross-entropy function to process the generated samples of conditional input and unconditional input. Loss3 is the loss function of the adversarial network.

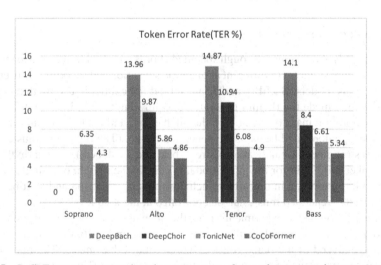

**Fig. 5.** CoCoFormer compares the token error rates of several current mainstream models.

Experiments have proven the effectiveness of improving the model: after adding the conditional chord model, the accuracy of the validation set increased by 1.11%, indicating that the model improved the quality of generated samples by adding extra information. Compared with the model that used relative positional attention in the second stage, the improved accuracy increased by 4.04%, indicating that chords combined with relative positions play a more obvious guiding role in note generation. The addition of extra information makes the sample generation closer to the data set samples, adding the rhythm information of the notes also conforms to this rule.

Improving the loss function is mainly aimed at generating samples more smoothly. Training under both unconditional and conditional inputs can enhance the stability of the model. Secondly, in order to alleviate the impact of teacher-forcing training on the diversity of sample generation, this paper set an adversarial loss function in training. Experiments have proven that using three loss functions for joint training can learn the potential expression of polyphonic music more effectively.

### 4.4  Comparative Test

This paper selects the main models currently used for polyphonic music generation and makes statistics on the token error rates(TER) of each part generation. As shown in Fig. 5. Due to the structure of the model, the soprano parts of DeepBach and DeepChoir are not involved in the generation and are set to 0. CoCoFormer achieved the best performance of these current models in the comparison results.

DeepBach, DeepChoir, and TonicNet are all models with RNN-based. Experiments proved that Transformer performs better in data set evaluation after solving the long-term dependency problem. It is worth noting that training samples of TonicNet expanded the data set to 1968 polyphonic music by transposing all pieces as many samples as possible, while CoCoFormer did not use any data augmentation methods.

### 4.5  Qualitative Experiment

Generating polyphonic music through specified chords and rhythms can make the generated music more suitable for different application scenarios and according to user needs. In the previous models, BachBot and TonicNet did not explicitly use rhythm condition as input, which made the rhythm generated uncontrollable. DeepBach and DeepChoir placed the duration mark of the note in the pitch event, and the beats events are related to the time signatures and beats of the generated music. (The rhythm of music input in 4/4 beat is strong beat, weak beat, sub-strong beat and weak beat). Such a rhythm event setting makes it difficult for the input model to control the rhythm of a single note. The rhythm coding proposed in this article includes the rest, extension and starting process of notes, so the generated music can be controlled at the note level.

This paper conducted experiments using the same melody input and different rhythm and chord conditions to analyze the output. As shown in Fig. 6, this paper performed a visually analyzed of the piano roll axis on an input 8-bar music. The main melody of the input remains unchanged. Only the texture is changed. The first line changes the input chord information and keeps the rhythm information unchanged. The experiment has shown that output notes keep the rhythm unchanged, and the harmony changes. The first column aligns the rhythm generated by the other three parts with the rhythm of the input melody, keeping the chord information unchanged and changing the rhythm of the generated sample texture. Experiments have proven that CoCoFormer can generate diversity based on given prompt information so that the same input melody can generate polyphonic music with different textures.

Figure 7 conducts a comparative experiment on whether to use the second stage of conditional encoding, gives an example of the score generated by Jasmine's chorus music. This paper specifies four voices to maintain a consistent rhythm. It can be seen that after adding conditional encoding, the generated music maintains better rhythmic and harmony consistency. In [33] we provide more music samples generated by CoCoFormer.

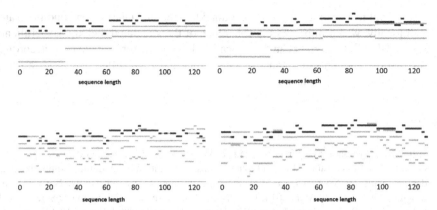

**Fig. 6.** Specify a melody and change the input chords and rhythm while keeping the melody. The upper left uses the melody's original chord and rhythm input, and the upper right changes the chord encoding while keeping the rhythm input unchanged. In the lower left, the input rhythm is consistent with the rhythm of the input melody, and the chords are unchanged. In the lower right, the chords and rhythm are also changed.

**Fig. 7.** The score of CoCoFormer under the specified conditional encoding with the melody of Jasmine and rhythm of are consistent. The left picture shows the generation using the second stage conditional coding. The right picture leaves the input conditional coding empty and only uses the backbone network for generation. Compared with the right picture, the left picture maintains a higher consistency in rhythm (the boxed part of the left picture), and the right picture has more wrong harmonies in the chord generation (the boxed part of the right picture)

## 5   Conclusions

Polyphonic music generation remains a challenging problem. This paper proposes CoCo-Former, which can not only better model polyphonic music but also have more control-lable texture generation. The model proposes a new attention mechanism so that chord and rhythm information can be explicitly and implicitly extracted by features. The loss function proposed in this paper is optimized through a combination of cross entropy and adversarial loss, and the network is trained to generate under given conditions and unconditionally, which improves the coherence of the generated melody. Experiments have proven that CoCoFormer can dynamically adjust the texture composition according to specified requirements and generate polyphonic music of different styles, showing good generalization performance.

# References

1. Hiller, L., Isaacson, L.: Experimental Music. McGraw-Hill, New York (1999)
2. Goel, K., Vohra, R., Sahoo, J.K.: Polyphonic music generation by modeling temporal dependencies using a RNN-DBN. In: Wermter, S., et al. (eds.) Artificial Neural Networks and Machine Learning – ICANN 2014. ICANN 2014. Lecture Notes in Computer Science, vol. 8681, pp. 217–224. Springer, Cham (2014). https://doi.org/10.1007/978-3-319-11179-7_28
3. Mangal, S., Modak, R., Joshi, P.: LSTM based music generation system. IARJSET., 47–54 (2019)
4. Keerti, G., Vaishnavi, A.N., Mukherjee, P., et al.: Attentional networks for music generation. Multimedia Tools Appl. **81**(4), 5179–5189 (2020)
5. Dong, H.-W., et al: MuseGAN: Multi-track sequential generative adversarial networks for symbolic music generation and accompaniment. In: Proceedings of the AAAI Conference on Artificial Intelligence (2022)
6. Vaswani, A., et al.: Attention is all you need. In: Neural Information Processing, vol. 30 (2017)
7. Huang, C.-Z., et al.: Music transformer. arXiv: Learning (2018)
8. MuseNet Homepage. https://openai.com/blog/musenet/. Accessed 5 May 2019
9. Lagler, K., et al.: GPT2: empirical slant delay model for radio space geodetic techniques. Geophys. Res. Lett. **40**(6), 1069–1073 (2013)
10. Johnson, D.D., Keller, R.M., Weintraut, N.: Learning to create Jazz melodies using a product of experts. In: ICCC (2017)
11. Hinton, G.E.: Products of experts. In: 9th International Conference on Artificial Neural Networks: ICANN '99, pp.1–6 (1999)
12. Yang, L.-C., Chou, S.-Y., Yang, Y.-H.: MidiNet: a convolutional generative adversarial network for symbolic-domain music generation. In: International Symposium/Conference on Music Information Retrieval (2017)
13. Boulanger-Lewandowski, N., Bengio, Y., Vincent, P.: Modeling temporal dependencies in high-dimensional sequences: application to polyphonic music generation and transcription. In: International Conference on Machine Learning (2012)
14. Peracha, O.: JS fake chorales: a synthetic dataset of polyphonic music with human annotation. In: CERN European Organization for Nuclear Research - Zenodo (2021)
15. Liang, F.: BachbBot: automatic composition in the style of Bach chorales. Univ. Camb. **8**, 19–48 (2016)
16. Hadjeres, G., Pachet, F., Nielsen, F.: DeepBach: a steerable model for bach chorales generation. arXiv: Artificial Intelligence (2016)
17. Peracha, O.: Improving polyphonic music models with feature-rich encoding. Cornell University - arXiv (2019)
18. Dey, R., Salem, F.M.: Gate-variants of gated recurrent unit (GRU) neural networks. arXiv: Neural and Evolutionary Computing (2017)
19. Lipton, Z.C., Berkowitz, J., Elkan, C.: A critical review of recurrent neural networks for sequence learning. arXiv: Learning (2015)

20. Todd, P.M.: A connectionist approach to algorithmic composition. Comput. Music J. **13**(4), 27–43 (1989)
21. Eck, D., Schmidhuber, J.: Finding temporal structure in music: blues improvisation with LSTM recurrent networks. In: Proceedings of the 12th IEEE Workshop on Neural Networks for Signal Processing, pp. 747–756 (2003)
22. Pascanu, R., et al.: How to construct deep recurrent neural networks.arXiv:1312.6026. Neural and Evolutionary Computing (2013)
23. Wu, S., Li, X., Sun, M.: Chord-conditioned melody harmonization with controllable Harmonicity. In: ICASSP 2023–2023 IEEE International Conference on Acoustics, Speech and Signal Processing (ICASSP), pp. 1–5 (2022)
24. Schuster, M., Paliwal, K.K.: Bidirectional recurrent neural networks. IEEE Trans. Signal Process. **45**(11), 2673–2681 (1997)
25. Tang, G., et al.: Why self-attention? A targeted evaluation of neural machine translation architectures. In: Proceedings of the 2018 Conference on Empirical Methods in Natural Language Processing (2018)
26. Donahue, C., et al.: LakhNES: improving multi-instrumental music generation with cross-domain pre-training. arXiv:1907.04868. Sound (2019)
27. Dai, Z., et al.: Transformer-XL: attentive language models beyond a fixed-length context. In: Proceedings of the 57th Annual Meeting of the Association for Computational Linguistics, pp. 2978–2988 (2019)
28. Donahue, C., Mao, H., McAuley, J.: The NES music database: a multi-instrumental dataset with expressive performance attributes. In: International Symposium/Conference on Music Information Retrieval (2018)
29. Radford, A., et al.: Language models are unsupervised multitask learners. OpenAI blog **1**(8), 9 (2019)
30. Zhang, W., et al.: Bridging the gap between training and inference for neural machine translation In: Proceedings of the Twenty-Ninth International Conference on International Joint Conferences on Artificial Intelligence, pp. 4790–4794 (2019)
31. Yang, Z., et al.: Unsupervised text style transfer using language models as discriminators. In: Proceedings of the 32nd International Conference on Neural Information Processing Systems, pp. 7298–7309 (2018)
32. Goodfellow, I., et al.: Generative adversarial nets. In: Proceedings of the 27th International Conference on Neural Information Processing Systems-Volume 2, pp. 2672–2680 (2014)
33. CoCoFormer Homepage. https://github.com/Zjy0401/CoCoFormer. Accessed 19 Nov 2023

# C2-MAGIC: Chord-Controllable Multi-track Accompaniment Generation with Interpretability and Creativity

Jingcheng Wu$^{(\boxtimes)}$ , Zihao Ji , and Pengfei Li

StarX, Beijing, China
jcwensta@gmail.com, 21830063@zju.edu.cn

**Abstract.** Musical notes are usually grouped into chords to generate aesthetically pleasing music, which is a special characteristic in symbolic music modeling. Good manipulation of chords not only brings harmony to music but also makes interactive music generation more manageable. However, prior attempts at chord-conditioned music generation have several limits: 1) Most previous work only considers chords as auxiliary tokens by adding them explicitly to the original conditional sequence, nevertheless, this simple design doesn't provide enough information and isn't capable of gaining good control over chords. 2) Some research reports good control of chords in terms of analogy but is limited under the context of single-track music of limited length. 3) Some achieve good matches of chords, yet at the cost of other evaluation metrics. To overcome these limits, we propose a novel architecture under the framework of multi-task learning, which additionally learns a latent chord representation used as extra contextual information for the multi-track accompaniment generation task. We evaluate our model both on the public LMD dataset and a private dataset of pop music. Experiments show that our model largely outperforms the state-of-the-art multi-track accompaniment generation model in terms of chord control ability and further improves the validation perplexity of the accompaniment generation task. Extensive objective and subjective studies also demonstrate the effectiveness of our approach. Furthermore, we show that our model brings extra interpretability and creativity through various inference experiments.

**Keywords:** Controllable music generation · Multi-task learning · Symbolic music

## 1 Introduction

Symbolic music modeling can be regarded as natural language processing of musical notes since music data (e.g., MIDI or XML format) can be represented as a sequence of discrete tokens. However, different from natural language, music has its own characteristics, among which chord is one of the most important.

© The Author(s), under exclusive license to Springer Nature Singapore Pte Ltd. 2024
X. Li et al. (Eds.): SOMI 2023, CCIS 2007, pp. 108–121, 2024.
https://doi.org/10.1007/978-981-97-0576-4_8

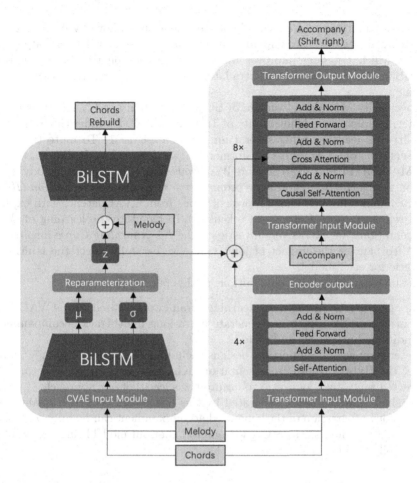

**Fig. 1.** The overall model architecture of our proposed multi-task training framework. The left part corresponds to the deep conditional generative model (CVAE). The right part corresponds to the encoder-decoder-based Transformer-XL model with separate memory for each side.

A chord consists of multiple musical notes that are heard as if playing simultaneously, which is the basis of harmony in music theory. In this work, we focus on generating multi-track accompaniment given melody and chord progressions.

Although many symbolic music generation models have taken chords into account, they each exhibit some limits from different aspects. Some previous works represent chords as explicit tokens and add them directly to the musical sequence as conditioning signals [7,9,10,14], which doesn't work well in controlling the given chord progressions. Other works either restrict their control ability to single-track music [2,4,17,20] or make a trade-off between good control ability and music quality [3].

In this paper, we address the challenges mentioned above by proposing C2-MAGIC, a multi-track accompaniment generation system with accurate chord control, which not only improves model performance on the accompaniment generation task but also brings extra interpretability and creativity with no side effects.

Specifically, we take advantage of the control ability of CVAE [16] and the long-term sequence modeling ability of Transformer-XL [5] under the framework of multi-task learning using several important designs: 1) To unite the input representation of CVAE and Transformer-XL, we design the *CVAE input module* with MuMIDI [14] and *Average Beat-Wise Embedding (ABWE)* for melody. 2) To gain better control over chords, we propose *Hybrid Chord Representation (HCR)* which combines implicit chord representations from CVAE latents with explicit chord representations from chord tokens. 3) To facilitate the learning of chord representations, we extensively investigate the *KL-Annealing Curve* inspired by [1]. 4) To balance the impact of joint tasks, we carefully select the multi-task loss ratio for each model.

In summary, the main contributions of this paper are as follows:

- We propose a multi-task learning framework based on CVAE and Transformer-XL, which can generate extra-long multi-track accompaniment conditioned on chords and melody.
- We employ several important designs including the new CAVE input module, the Hybrid Chord Representation, KL-Annealing Curve, and carefully selected multi-task loss ratio to ensure the success of our approach.
- We show that the music generated by this framework is of high quality and the chord progression of the generated accompaniment can be fully controlled by the input chords. Moreover, we manifest that our model brings extra interpretability and creativity.

## 2    Related Work

Chord-conditioned music generation can be considered a seq2seq task whose conditions are changed over time. The most common approach is to model the conditional probability: $p(music|condition)$ [17]. In brief, two methods have been used in recent works to tackle chord-conditioned music generation. The first is *explicit representation* method, i.e., chord classes are added directly to the original musical sequence as conditional tokens [7,9,10,14]. The second is *implicit representation* method, i.e., a latent representation of chords is learned by neural networks and then mixed with the music sequence by concatenating or adding operation [2,17].

The current MIDI tokenization methods, such as MIDI-like [15], MuMIDI [14], REMI [10], and Compound Word [9], all use chord tokens in an explicit manner, which forces the Transformer to learn the connection between chords and notes automatically by attention mechanism. However, this design relies heavily on the ability of the model itself and is insufficient in obtaining good control results over chord progressions, especially in low-resource cases. As for the work using latent chord representation, limited by its music tokenization method and the design of the music generation model, the results are restricted to short segments of single-track music [2,4,17,20] or sacrifice musical quality [3]. To our knowledge, our work is the first to use hybrid chord representation to gain accurate control of chords and is able to generate polyphonic music with arbitrary lengths of multiple tracks without any side effects.

## 3  Method

### 3.1  Model Overview

The overall model architecture is shown in Fig. 1, which adopts a multi-task learning framework based on CVAE [16] and Transformer-XL [5]. The CVAE part aims at learning a smooth latent space containing chord information by chords reconstruction task, while the Transformer-XL part focuses on accompaniment modeling with extra contextual information from the latent space. Further details are described below.

### 3.2  CVAE Input Module

The illustration of CVAE input module is shown in Fig. 2. Unlike previous works, we don't use piano roll representation for two reasons. On one hand, piano roll suffers from sparseness and is unstable to train [6]; on the other hand, it is different in nature from the MuMIDI representation that is used in the accompaniment modeling task. To be specific, as is shown in Fig. 2 and Eq. 1, each beat of music corresponds to a chord token and several [pitch, duration] token pairs representing note information in the melody, sharing the same vocabulary used in accompaniment modeling task. As the number of notes in each beat may be different, we adopt a padding token to make each beat the same length. Then, the melody tokens and chord tokens are passed to different embedding layers. As there are multiple tokens for melody in each beat, we average the embedding of the tokens within the same beat, which we call as *Average Beat-Wise Embedding*(ABWE) for short. The final input is the linear projection of the concatenation of chord embedding and melody average embedding:

$$\mathcal{X}_{\text{cvae}} = \mathcal{W}_{\text{proj}}(\mathcal{W}_c \oplus \mathcal{W}_{\text{avg}}[\mathcal{P}_1, \mathcal{D}_1 \cdots \mathcal{P}_n, \mathcal{D}_n]) \tag{1}$$

### 3.3  KL-Annealing Curve

To introduce the KL-Annealing Curve, we first briefly recap the CVAE model. Given $m$ as melody, $c$ as chord, $z$ as the latent variable, $p_\theta(z|m, c)$ as the true posterior, $q_\phi(z|m, c)$ as the approximated posterior, we aim to maximize the conditional likelihood $p_\theta(c|m, z)$. The original problem is intractable, however,

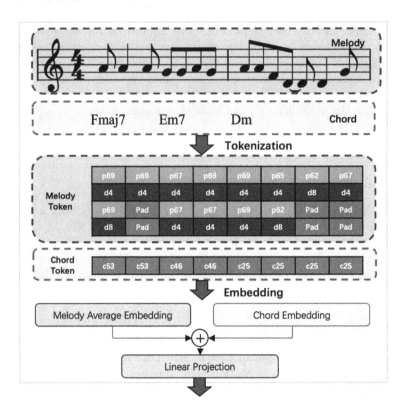

**Fig. 2.** The input module of CVAE model. The example melody consists of 2 bars containing 13 notes, which is 8 beats with time signature 4/4. In this case, Fmaj7, Em7, Dm chord lasts for 2, 2, and 4 beats respectively.

under the framework of Stochastic Gradient Variational Bayes (SGVB) [11], we can instead maximize the evidence lower bound (ELBO) which is written as:

$$\mathcal{L}_{\text{cvae}} = \mathbb{E}_{q_\phi(z|m,c)}[log p_\theta(c|m,z)] - \\ \mathbf{KL}(q_\phi(z|m,c)||p_\theta(z|m)) \tag{2}$$

Maximizing the ELBO is equivalent to minimizing the negative ELBO, hence, the loss function consists of two parts: the chord reconstruction loss $\mathcal{L}_{\text{chord}}$ and KL divergence loss $\mathcal{L}_{\text{KL}}$:

$$\mathcal{L}_{\text{cvae}} = \mathcal{L}_{\text{chord}} + \beta \cdot \mathcal{L}_{\text{KL}} \tag{3}$$

where $\beta$ is a penalty term that balances the music information embedded in the latent space and the structure of this space, $\mathcal{L}_{\text{KL}}$ is formulated as a closed form without estimation under Gaussian latent variable assumption

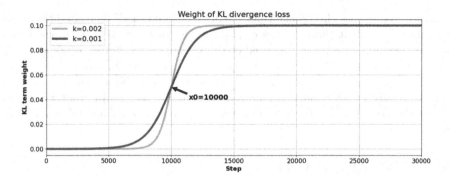

**Fig. 3.** The annealing curve of kl loss weight $\beta$. This example shows the difference between k=0.002 and k=0.001 when $x_0 = 10000$ and $\beta_{max} = 0.1$.

following [11] and $\mathcal{L}_{\text{chord}}$ is defined as the Negative Log Likelihood Loss (NLL) taken between the CVAE decoder outputs and the ground-truth chord tokens:

$$\mathcal{L}_{\text{chord}} = -\frac{1}{L}\sum_{l=1}^{L} log(p_\theta(\boldsymbol{c}|\boldsymbol{m}, \boldsymbol{z}^{(l)})), \tag{4}$$

$$\boldsymbol{z}^{(l)} = \boldsymbol{\mu}^{(l)} + \boldsymbol{\sigma}^{(l)} \odot \epsilon^{(l)}, \epsilon^{(l)} \sim \mathcal{N}(\boldsymbol{0}, \boldsymbol{I})$$

Inspired by [1], we perform a sigmoid annealing strategy over $\beta$ to preserve enough useful information in the latent variable $z$. Formally:

$$\beta = \frac{\beta_{\text{max}}}{1 + e^{-k \cdot (\text{step} - x_0)}} \tag{5}$$

As is shown in Fig. 3, $k$ controls the shape of the curve, and $x_0$ determines the transition point where half of $\beta_{\text{max}}$ is reached. At the early stage of training, $\beta$ is nearly zero, focusing on the reconstruction work. Then as training progresses, $\beta$ gradually increases to a maximum weight $\beta_{\text{max}}$, trying to smooth the latent space for a good structure. Experiments show that the choice of KL-Annealing-Curve is important to the final model performance, which we will discuss more in later sections.

### 3.4   Hybrid Chord Representation

Previous work simply adopts *explicit chord tokens* as control conditions without providing enough contextual information. Consequently, it's hard for the transformer decoder to learn how to organize multi-track notes with the given chord progression. To get better control over chords, we introduce a learning-based *latent chord representation* as extra context information. We call the combination of explicit chord tokens and the learning-base latent chord representation as *Hybrid Chord Representation (HCR)*, which can be described as follows:

$$\begin{cases} \text{Encoder} : e_i = q_\Psi(\boldsymbol{m}_i, \boldsymbol{c}_i, M_i^E) \\ \text{Decoder} : y_j = p_\Theta(y_{t<j}, (e_i \oplus q_\phi(\boldsymbol{z}_i|\boldsymbol{m}_i, \boldsymbol{c}_i)), M_j^D) \end{cases} \tag{6}$$

where $e_i$ represents the transformer encoder outputs of $i^{th}$ bar conditioned on melody $\boldsymbol{m}_i$, explicit chord tokens $\boldsymbol{c}_i$ and encoder memory $M_i^E$. Then the transformer decoder outputs $y_j$ are predicted using previous-steps tokens $y_{t<j}$, the encoder outputs $e_i$ alone with the approximated posterior samples from the latent space $q_\phi(\boldsymbol{z}_i|\boldsymbol{m}_i, \boldsymbol{c}_i)$ and the decoder memory $M_j^D$. Note that $q_\phi(\boldsymbol{z}_i|\boldsymbol{m}_i, \boldsymbol{c}_i)$ is concatenated with $e_i$ on the dimension of sentence length. In other words, the latent variable $\boldsymbol{z}_i$ acts like "extra" tokens which represent the high-level chord information.

### 3.5 Multi-task Loss Ratio

Our training objective is defined as follows:

$$\mathcal{L}_{\mathrm{mt}} = \mathcal{L}_{\mathrm{mel2accom}} + \gamma \cdot \mathcal{L}_{\mathrm{cvae}} \tag{7}$$

$$\mathcal{L}_{\mathrm{mel2accom}} = \mathcal{L}_{\mathrm{token}} + \alpha \cdot \mathcal{L}_{\mathrm{vel\_dur}} \tag{8}$$

where $\gamma$ controls the relative importance between the melody-to-accompaniment modeling task loss $\mathcal{L}_{\mathrm{mel2accom}}$ and the latent space learning task loss $\mathcal{L}_{\mathrm{cvae}}$ defined in Eq. 3. To be more specific, we use a compression-expansion trick [9,14,19] to model different attributes (pitch, velocity, and duration) of a note with different heads separately. $\mathcal{L}_{\mathrm{mel2accom}}$ consists of two parts: the main token loss $\mathcal{L}_{\mathrm{token}}$ and the velocity-duration loss $\mathcal{L}_{\mathrm{vel\_dur}}$ by calculating NLL of tokens of certain types, with $\alpha$ being a factor that regulates the impact of different types of tokens. We set $\alpha$ as 0.2 in our experiments.

## 4 Experiments

### 4.1 Experimental Settings

**Datasets.** We train and evaluate our model on two MIDI datasets: the public Lakh MIDI dataset (LMD) [13] and a private dataset of pop music. For a fair comparison, we follow the data collection pipeline of PopMAG [14] on the pop music subset of LMD. In addition, we collect a private dataset of 6806 multi-track midis of pop music (247 h) with a time signature of 4/4 after extensive manual verification and annotations.

**Vocabulary.** We use MuMIDI as the base tokenization method. We choose a total of 8 common chords, including 4 triads (major, minor, augmented, diminished) and 4 sevenths (dominant sevenths, major sevenths, minor sevenths, half-diminished sevenths). Combined with 12 chroma (C, C#, D, D#, E, F, F#, G, Ab, A, Bb, B), the total number of chord tokens is 96. We use 128 pitch tokens, 92 bar index tokens, 32 duration bins, 32 velocity bins, and 32 position bins. Instrument tokens include Piano, Bass, Drum, Guitar, String, and one specially for the melody.

## Model Configurations

*CVAE Model Setting.* We set the melody embedding size, chord embedding size, linear projection size and latent vector size to 512, 256, 512, 512, respectively. Each BiLSTM module contains two layers of hidden size 512.

*Transformer-XL Model Setting.* Encoder layer, decoder layer, encoder heads and decoder heads are set to 4, 8, 8, 8, respectively. In order to shorten the model training time, we set the maximum sequence length of the input model to 384. In addition, we set memory length to 512 to keep contextual information.

**Training and Inference Setup.** We train our model using one Tesla V100 GPU with a batch size of 32. We use the Adam optimizer to update the model with parameters $\beta_1 = 0.9$, $\beta_2 = 0.98$, $\epsilon = 10^{-9}$. The learning rate is updated using the CosineAnnealing strategy [12] with an initial value of $2.5*10^{-4}$. It takes 200k steps for training until convergence. For Inference, we input a melody to the model along with its corresponding chord. To ensure the diversity of generated musical pieces, we use top-k sampling, temperature sampling, and hidden space sampling, where $k = 5$ and *temperature* $= 1.2$.

## Evaluation Metrics

*Objective Evaluation.* We follow the same design as PopMAG [14] for a fair comparison. In brief, $CA$ measures the Chord Accuracy between the generated accompaniment and the input chords, PPL means perplexity which is widely used in sequence modeling, while $\mathcal{D}_P$, $\mathcal{D}_V$, $\mathcal{D}_D$ and $\mathcal{D}_{IOI}$ measures the similarity between the generated samples and ground truths in terms of pitch, velocity, duration, and rhythm.

*Subjective Evaluation.* We randomly select 22 MIDIs as ground truth from test set and extract the melody of each MIDI. These melodies are then used to generate their corresponding accompaniments using PopMAG, C2-MAGIC with given chord and default chord from ground truth, respectively. 11 professionals and 26 music novices are asked to perform the subjective evaluation using a 5-point scale. Questions include: 1) How much they like the music? 2) How harmonious the music is? 3) Is the music creative?

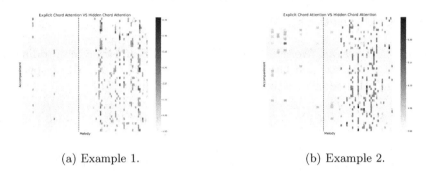

(a) Example 1.                          (b) Example 2.

**Fig. 4.** Attention visualization of explicit chord tokens and latent chord representations. The figure is drawn using the average attention score of all heads in the last layer of encoder-decoder attention in the Transformer-XL model.

**Table 1.** Objective results of comparison between our model and PopMAG on LMD dataset. The best result of each metric is marked in bold.

| Model | CA ↑ | PPL ↓ | $\mathcal{D}_P$ ↑ | $\mathcal{D}_V$ ↑ | $\mathcal{D}_D$ ↑ | $\mathcal{D}_{IOI}$ ↑ |
|---|---|---|---|---|---|---|
| PopMAG[14] | $0.647^{\pm0.013}$ | 1.131 | $0.602^{\pm0.012}$ | $0.454^{\pm0.007}$ | $0.478^{\pm0.010}$ | $0.688^{\pm0.007}$ |
| Ours | $\mathbf{0.925^{\pm0.009}}$ | **1.127** | $\mathbf{0.652^{\pm0.011}}$ | $\mathbf{0.504^{\pm0.008}}$ | $\mathbf{0.512^{\pm0.007}}$ | $0.692^{\pm0.009}$ |

### 4.2   Results

**Comparison with Previous Works.** As is shown in Table 1, our model outperforms PopMAG in respect of almost all objective metrics, especially *Chord Accuracy*, where we see a great improvement of 27.8%. The results indicate that our model not only obtains strong control over chords but also further improves model fitness in the accompaniment generation task. The results can be explained in two folds. First, we add learning-based chord representation as contextual information, which makes it easier for the transformer decoder to learn the relations between chords and notes from multiple tracks. Second, our model is under the framework of multi-task learning and the chord reconstruction task conditioned on melody is a related task to the accompaniment generation task. By sharing related information, the model performance is further improved. In consideration of baseline diversity, we particularly note that [4] and [20] report chord accuracy of 72.53% and 82.25% on *single-track monophonic* music generation task, respectively. While we achieve 92.5% (see Table 1) chord accuracy on *multi-track polyphonic* music generation task.

### Method Analyses

*Study of CVAE Input Module.* We try summation and average of embeddings for the CVAE input module. It is observed that Averaged Beat-Wise Embedding performs slightly better. However, if we change the input representation to piano

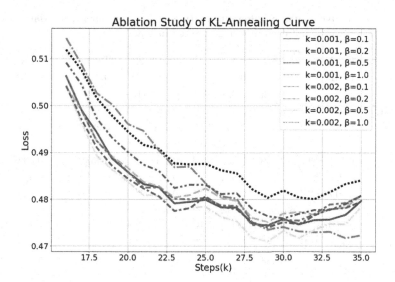

(a) Ablation study of KL-annealing curve.

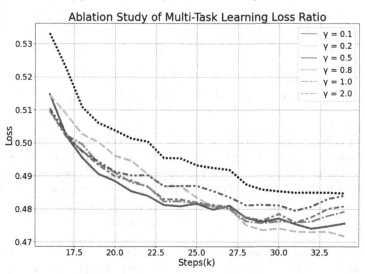

(b) Ablation study of multi-task learning loss ratio.

**Fig. 5.** We try different combinations of $k$ and $\beta_{\max}$ while keeping $\gamma = 0.2$ and other configurations the same. We vary the coefficient of CVAE model loss $\gamma$ with $k = 0.002$ and $\beta_{\max} = 0.1$.

**Table 2.** Objective results of different ablation settings on our private dataset of pop music. The best result of each metric is marked in bold.

| Settings | CA ↑ | NLL ↓ | $\mathcal{D}_P$ ↑ | $\mathcal{D}_V$ ↑ | $\mathcal{D}_D$ ↑ | $\mathcal{D}_{IOI}$ ↑ |
|---|---|---|---|---|---|---|
| Best | **$0.934^{\pm 0.012}$** | **0.453** | **$0.621^{\pm 0.012}$** | **$0.481^{\pm 0.008}$** | **$0.478^{\pm 0.009}$** | **$0.651^{\pm 0.007}$** |
| Study of CVAE Input Module | | | | | | |
| SBWE | $0.912^{\pm 0.013}$ | 0.457 | $0.592^{\pm 0.012}$ | $0.431^{\pm 0.028}$ | $0.457^{\pm 0.012}$ | $0.626^{\pm 0.004}$ |
| Piano roll | $0.428^{\pm 0.034}$ | 0.479 | $0.332^{\pm 0.003}$ | $0.301^{\pm 0.023}$ | $0.287^{\pm 0.012}$ | $0.494^{\pm 0.023}$ |
| Study of KL-Annealing Strategy | | | | | | |
| $\beta = 0.1$ | $0.921^{\pm 0.012}$ | 0.469 | $0.581^{\pm 0.026}$ | $0.446^{\pm 0.021}$ | $0.458^{\pm 0.003}$ | $0.632^{\pm 0.012}$ |
| $\beta = 0.2$ | $0.928^{\pm 0.016}$ | 0.462 | $0.594^{\pm 0.009}$ | $0.458^{\pm 0.035}$ | $0.461^{\pm 0.005}$ | $0.643^{\pm 0.018}$ |
| $\beta = 0.5$ | $0.917^{\pm 0.033}$ | 0.474 | $0.569^{\pm 0.011}$ | $0.432^{\pm 0.008}$ | $0.446^{\pm 0.021}$ | $0.625^{\pm 0.006}$ |
| Study of Hybrid Chord Representations | | | | | | |
| Latent | $0.729^{\pm 0.051}$ | 0.468 | $0.423^{\pm 0.018}$ | $0.361^{\pm 0.023}$ | $0.353^{\pm 0.009}$ | $0.498^{\pm 0.017}$ |
| Explicit | $0.632^{\pm 0.017}$ | 0.482 | $0.372^{\pm 0.020}$ | $0.322^{\pm 0.044}$ | $0.309^{\pm 0.015}$ | $0.432^{\pm 0.023}$ |
| Neither | – | 0.483 | $0.377^{\pm 0.012}$ | $0.319^{\pm 0.031}$ | $0.301^{\pm 0.024}$ | $0.419^{\pm 0.005}$ |

**Fig. 6.** Demo analysis by professional composers.

roll which is frequently used in VAE-based symbolic music generation models [3,18], there is an obvious decline in model performance, which demonstrates the effectiveness of our proposed CVAE input module. We speculate that this is due to the different nature of data presentations. Our CVAE input module uses the same vocabulary and midi representations as the accompaniment generation task, therefore, it is a more consistent task than using piano roll representations.

*Study of KL-Annealing Curve.* As shown in Table 2, if we set $\beta$ as constant, there will be an apparent decline in objective metrics, illustrating the importance of KL-Annealing Curve. Furthermore, to study the influence of different KL-Annealing curves, we compare different pairs of $k$ and $\beta_{max}$. Results shown in Fig. 5(a) indicate that $k = 0.002$ generally performs better compared with $k = 0.001$. We suspect that this is because the training of Transformer-XL hasn't been sufficient yet when CVAE loss is introduced at an early stage for $k = 0.001$. It is also observed in Fig. 5(a) that a smaller $\beta_{max}$ is preferred in general, which is consistent with the observations when $\beta$ is constant.

*Study of Hybrid Chord Representations.* To investigate the effectiveness of our Hybrid Chord Representations, we conduct ablation studies on chord conditions.

**Table 3.** Subjective results of human evaluations for Ground Truth, PopMAG, C2-MAGIC with Given Chord and Default Chord, respectively. O: Overall, H: Harmony, C: Creativity, $P_x$: p-value of t-test with PopMAG for each metric. The results with statistical significance at 95% confidence level are marked in bold.

| Setting | O | H | C | $P_O$ | $P_H$ | $P_C$ |
|---|---|---|---|---|---|---|
| All Participants | | | | | | |
| GT | 3.44 | 3.40 | 3.36 | – | – | – |
| PopMAG | 2.61 | 2.46 | 2.92 | – | – | – |
| Ours+GC | 2.84 | 2.73 | 2.99 | 0.09 | 0.07 | 0.36 |
| Ours+DC | 2.86 | **2.74** | 3.02 | 0.07 | **0.04** | 0.13 |
| Professionals | | | | | | |
| GT | 3.38 | 3.25 | 3.11 | – | – | – |
| PopMAG | 2.13 | 1.95 | 2.38 | – | – | – |
| Ours+GC | 2.46 | **2.36** | 2.48 | 0.09 | **0.04** | 0.48 |
| Ours+DC | **2.57** | 2.31 | **2.62** | **0.05** | 0.08 | **0.05** |

From Table 2, it can be seen that using only explicit chord tokens makes very limited contributions to model performance. However, using only the latent chord representations gives much better results, which demonstrates the advantage of the leaning-based chord representations. It is also noticeable that combining the explicit chord tokens with the latent representations leads to even better results, showing the superiority of Hybrid Chord Representations.

*Study of Multi-task Loss Ratio.* To reveal the influence of multi-task loss ratio, we vary the coefficient of CVAE loss $\gamma$. It can be seen that $\gamma$ is of vital importance on model performance, where model performance tends to improve with smaller $\gamma$. The results indicate that although the CVAE model is helpful to the accompaniment generation task, overemphasis of CVAE loss will result in degeneration of performance.

### 4.3   Further Discussion

**Model Interpretability.** To better highlight the effectiveness of latent chord representations, we visualize the encoder-decoder attention heatmap in Fig. 4. It is shown that the attention score of latent chord representations is not only more dense but also more diverse than explicit chord tokens, which indicates that the accompaniment has a much stronger correlation with latent chord representations.

**Model Creativity.** The inference diversity of Transformer-based models relies on stochastic sampling [8], which suffers from error accumulation due to the autoregressive mechanism. In contrast, we show that our architecture brings extra creativity by latent space sampling, which is proven by subjective evaluations in Table 3. As shown in Fig. 6, given a chord progression, the generated multi-track accompaniments are fully controlled by the conditions and we can see automatic chord inversions and perfect rhythm coherence among different tracks.

### 4.4  Human Evaluation

It can be seen from Table 3 that our model achieves better overall results than PopMAG in every aspect. As for harmony, we have achieved better results in all groups due to good control of input chords. As for creativity, our model scores better than PopMAG, especially in the professional group under the default chord setting, but it lacks statistical significance in other groups. We argue that the judgment of creativity largely depends on personal music experience and requires professional musical knowledge to tell the subtle differences between music pieces. It's also worth mentioning that the quality of generated samples is still below the ground truth. According to listeners' feedback, this is mainly because our model can only generate accompaniments containing 5 instruments (the same as PopMAG and MuseGAN), making the music less contagious. We plan to remove the instrument limits in future work to further improve generation quality.

## 5  Conclusion

In this work, we have proposed C2-MAGIC, a chord-controllable multi-track accompaniment generation system, which incorporates CVAE and Transformer-XL under the framework of multi-task learning. We adopt several important measures to ensure the success of our method, including the new CAVE input module, the Hybrid Chord Representation, KL-Annealing Curve and carefully-selected multi-task loss ratio. Experiments show that our model not only achieves much stronger chord control but also improves model performance, both on the public LMD dataset and a private dataset. We further show interpretability through attention visualization and creativity by human evaluations as bonus advantage for our proposition. For future work, we will extend our architecture to accurately control other important musical factors like texture and style for multi-track polyphonic music and remove instrument limits to further improve generation quality.

## References

1. Bowman, S.R., Vilnis, L., Vinyals, O., Dai, A., Jozefowicz, R., Bengio, S.: Generating sentences from a continuous space. In: Proceedings of The 20th SIGNLL Conference on Computational Natural Language Learning, pp. 10–21. Association for Computational Linguistics, Berlin, Germany (2016). https://doi.org/10.18653/v1/K16-1002, https://aclanthology.org/K16-1002

2. Brunner, G., Wang, Y., Wattenhofer, R., Wiesendanger, J.: JamBot: music theory aware chord based generation of polyphonic music with LSTMS. In: 2017 IEEE 29th International Conference on Tools with Artificial Intelligence (ICTAI). pp. 519–526. IEEE (2017)

3. Chen, Y.W., Lee, H.S., Chen, Y.H., Wang, H.M.: SurpriseNet: melody harmonization conditioning on user-controlled surprise contours. arXiv preprint: arXiv:2108.00378 (2021)

4. Choi, K., Park, J., Heo, W., Jeon, S., Park, J.: Chord conditioned melody generation with transformer based decoders. IEEE Access 9, 42071–42080 (2021)

5. Dai, Z., Yang, Z., Yang, Y., Carbonell, J., Le, Q.V., Salakhutdinov, R.: Transformer-XL: attentive language models beyond a fixed-length context. arXiv preprint: arXiv:1901.02860 (2019)

6. Donahue, C., Mao, H.H., Li, Y.E., Cottrell, G.W., McAuley, J.: LakhNES: improving multi-instrumental music generation with cross-domain pre-training. arXiv preprint: arXiv:1907.04868 (2019)

7. Genchel, B., Pati, A., Lerch, A.: Explicitly conditioned melody generation: a case study with interdependent RNNs. arXiv preprint: arXiv:1907.05208 (2019)

8. Holtzman, A., Buys, J., Du, L., Forbes, M., Choi, Y.: The curious case of neural text degeneration. arXiv preprint: arXiv:1904.09751 (2019)

9. Hsiao, W.Y., Liu, J.Y., Yeh, Y.C., Yang, Y.H.: Compound word transformer: learning to compose full-song music over dynamic directed hypergraphs. In: Proceedings of the AAAI Conference on Artificial Intelligence, vol. 35, pp. 178–186 (2021)

10. Huang, Y.S., Yang, Y.H.: Pop music transformer: beat-based modeling and generation of expressive pop piano compositions. In: Proceedings of the 28th ACM International Conference on Multimedia, pp. 1180–1188 (2020)

11. Kingma, D.P., Welling, M.: Auto-encoding variational Bayes. arXiv preprint: arXiv:1312.6114 (2013)

12. Loshchilov, I., Hutter, F.: SGDR: gradient descent with warm restarts. arXiv preprint: arXiv:1608.03983 (2016)

13. Raffel, C.: Learning-based methods for comparing sequences, with applications to audio-to-midi alignment and matching. Columbia University (2016)

14. Ren, Y., He, J., Tan, X., Qin, T., Zhao, Z., Liu, T.Y.: PopMAG: pop music accompaniment generation. In: Proceedings of the 28th ACM International Conference on Multimedia, pp. 1198–1206 (2020)

15. Simon, I., Oore, S.: Performance RNN: generating music with expressive timing and dynamics. Magenta Blog, p. 16 (2017)

16. Sohn, K., Lee, H., Yan, X.: Learning structured output representation using deep conditional generative models. In: Advances in Neural Information Processing Systems, vol. 28 (2015)

17. Wang, Z., Wang, D., Zhang, Y., Xia, G.: Learning interpretable representation for controllable polyphonic music generation. arXiv preprint: arXiv:2008.07122 (2020)

18. Yang, R., Wang, D., Wang, Z., Chen, T., Jiang, J., Xia, G.: Deep music analogy via latent representation disentanglement. arXiv preprint: arXiv:1906.03626 (2019)

19. Zeng, M., Tan, X., Wang, R., Ju, Z., Qin, T., Liu, T.Y.: MusicBERT: symbolic music understanding with large-scale pre-training. arXiv preprint: arXiv:2106.05630 (2021)

20. Zhu, H., et al.: Xiaoice band: A melody and arrangement generation framework for pop music. In: Proceedings of the 24th ACM SIGKDD International Conference on Knowledge Discovery & Data Mining, pp. 2837–2846 (2018)

# HRPE: Hierarchical Relative Positional Encoding for Transformer-Based Structured Symbolic Music Generation

Pengfei Li$^{(\boxtimes)}$ ⓘ, Jingcheng Wuⓘ, and Zihao Jiⓘ

StarX, Beijing, China
pfli9411@gmail.com, 21830063@zju.edu.cn

**Abstract.** Musicians often structure their compositions hierarchically to imbue their music with rich expressiveness. As a result, generating musically meaningful music with well-organized structures has been a significant research goal for many scholars. Several approaches have been proposed to achieve this objective, typically involving multi-step generation pipelines or sophisticated model architectures based on domain knowledge, which can increase model complexity and generalization difficulty. In this study, we demonstrate that a hierarchical positional encoding adapted for music is sufficient to enhance model performance and generate coherent music with hierarchical structures. We incorporate hierarchical positional information into the Transformer model by modifying the attention matrix with relative position bias at different levels, enabling the model to learn long-short-term dependencies jointly and become less sensitive to positional shifts of several notes. Additionally, we investigate the design of section-level relative positional encoding through ablation studies. To validate our approach, we annotate two datasets (POP909-S and POP2000-S) with music sections and present evidence for both single-track monophonic music and multi-track polyphonic music generation tasks. Experimental results demonstrate that our approach outperforms state-of-the-art Transformer models in both subjective and objective evaluations. We plan to release the source code and annotated datasets upon acceptance.

**Keywords:** Hierarchical relative position · Music structure · Symbolic music

## 1 Introduction

Transformer-based models have demonstrated remarkable achievements in symbolic music generation, as they excel in handling global structures [2,6,8,12–14,20,22,25]. However, generating music with musically meaningful and coherent structures remains a challenge, as music is inherently organized according to aesthetic principles.

To tackle this issue, prior research has attempted to decompose the generation process into multiple steps or employ intricate model architectures combined

X. Li et al. (Eds.): SOMI 2023, CCIS 2007, pp. 122–134, 2024.
https://doi.org/10.1007/978-981-97-0576-4_9

with domain expertise [3,21,25]. Though significant strides have been made in enhancing the structure of generated music, these approaches increase model complexity and are not readily generalizable to other domains. We posit that the difficulty in generating well-structured music with Transformers primarily stems from two factors. Firstly, prior Transformer-like architectures have not implemented appropriate positional encoding for music. For instance, token-level relative positional encoding solely considers the relative distance between tokens, neglecting to explicitly model the high-level correlations within musical bars and sections. Secondly, high-quality data with structural annotations is scarce, hampering the learning of meaningful musical structures.

In response, we present **H**ierarchical **R**elative **P**osi-tional **E**ncoding (HRPE), an innovative positional encoding technique tailored for structured music generation. Specifically, we adjust the attention matrix directly by incorporating bias from the relative distance embedding of distinct tokens at the bar and section levels. As a plugin operation requiring minimal modifications to the Transformer architecture, this method is easily generalizable to other contexts with distinct definitions of 'bar' and 'section.' To showcase our approach, we manually annotate sections in two datasets: the publicly available POP909 dataset and an internal multi-track music dataset of 2,000 pop songs, which we dub POP909-S and POP2000-S, respectively. We subsequently compare various positional encoding methods on single-track monophonic music and multi-track polyphonic music generation tasks using these two datasets. While our current experiments focus on pop music due to its relatively clear and definable sections, we intend to expand our methods to other music genres in future work.

Experimental outcomes corroborate that our proposed HRPE consistently enhances model performance in both objective and subjective evaluations. Moreover, imposing hierarchical bias on the attention matrix allows the model to converge to the optimal point with fewer training steps, offering an added benefit. In summary, our contributions include:

- A novel positional encoding technique that integrates hierarchical information in music, effectively augmenting model performance and generating coherent music with hierarchical structures. This approach is also generalizable to other domains.
- A comprehensive investigation of diverse positional encoding methods on single-track and multi-track music generation tasks.
- Two music datasets with precise section annotations that will aid future research on structured music generation.

## 2    Related Work

### 2.1    Structured Symbolic Music Generation

The generation of music with well-defined structures has been a topic of interest in recent years. Prior solutions have relied on either decomposing the generation process or utilizing complex model architectures in conjunction with domain knowledge. For instance, some works have first generated frameworks, skeletons, or structures, and subsequently produced complete music based on these conditions [3,21,25]. Others have generated complete music pieces under constraints and then refined them using neural networks [16,24]. Alternatively, some approaches have incorporated texture and form related to harmony to learn the structure of music [23]. In contrast, we propose a method that solely employs HRPE and can generate music with well-organized structures. Our approach has been validated not only on single-track monophonic music (melody) but also on multi-track polyphonic music.

## 2.2 Positional Information in Transformer

The Transformer model is inherently permutation invariant, making the integration of positional information in sequence modeling a lively research area [7]. Common positional encoding techniques include **A**bsolute **P**ositional **E**ncoding (APE) and **R**elative **P**ositional **E**ncoding (RPE). For instance, the original Transformer [18] used sinusoidal APE to represent the absolute position of tokens. Segatron [1] adopted a combined positional encoding of paragraph, sentence, and token by modifying the input word embeddings. To better capture the relative order of tokens, RPE and many variants have been studied in recent years [2,5,10,13,15,17]. Our proposed HRPE can be seen as a variant of RPE in which musical structures on different timescales are considered jointly.

## 3     Methodology

This section provides a detailed description of the model architecture and its fundamental components. Specifically, Section A provides a brief overview of the model, highlighting important aspects such as data representations, input and output modules, and the integration of hierarchical relative positional encoding. Subsequently, Section B and Section C delve into the two critical components of the model, namely bar-level and section-level relative positional encoding, expounding on their respective designs and implementations.

### 3.1     Model Overview

**Single-Track and Multi-track Representations.** In this section, we present the music representations employed in our proposed method. To address our tasks and minimize sequence length, we adopt a modified version of the Compound Word representation [12]. Importantly, we note that our approach is generic and not reliant on specific data representations. As illustrated in the Input Module diagram in Fig. 1, a Compound Word representation consists of several components, including type, bar-beat, pitch, duration, and velocity. For the single-track representation, we exclude the chord and tempo fields from the original Compound Word implementation and include start-end pairs of structure in the [type] category to maintain end-structure-followed-by-start-structure

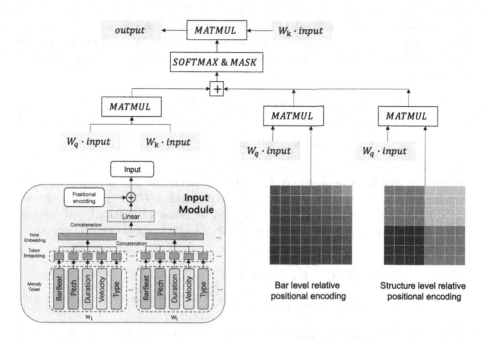

**Fig. 1.** An illustration of the attention module with hierarchical structure information, where the structure information includes Bar-RPE and Section-RPE.

patterns. The start-end pairs of structures explicitly indicate the segmentation of notes corresponding to changes in music sections. For the multi-track representation, we introduce instrument tokens as additional attributes of notes, as described in [6], but we exclude instrument tokens in the type category.

**Input Module and Output Module.** The input module and output module utilized in our proposed method are similar to those of the Compound Word Transformer [12]. In the input module, we first map the various elements of Compound Word into different embeddings $\mathcal{P}_{t,k}$ and concatenate them. Subsequently, these embeddings are mapped to the input dimension of the model using the projection matrix $\mathcal{W}_{\text{in}}$. This process can be represented as follows:

$$X = \mathcal{W}_{\text{in}}[\mathcal{P}_{t,1} \oplus \cdots \oplus \mathcal{P}_{t,k}], k = 1, \ldots, K \tag{1}$$

However, our approach differs from Compound Word Transformer in three ways. First, we replace absolute positional encoding with hierarchical relative positional encoding. Second, we add section-related tokens to the type class to explicitly indicate the segmentation of notes as the music section changes. Third, for the multi-track experiments, we add [instrument] to the Compound Word to distinguish between different tracks.

In the output module, we follow the two-stage settings in the Compound Word Transformer. Initially, we predict [type] and re-encode it as $E_{ft}$. Then, we concatenate $E_{ft}$ with the final hidden layer states $\mathcal{H}_t$ to predict the other elements. This process can be represented as follows, where $\mathcal{W}_k$ and $\mathcal{W}_f$ are weight matrices corresponding to the various elements, and Sample is the sampling function:

$$
\begin{aligned}
E_{ft} &= \text{Embedding}_{\text{f}}(\text{Sample}_f(\text{Softmax}(\mathcal{W}_{\text{f}}\mathcal{H}_{\text{t}}))) \\
H_o &= \mathcal{W}_{\text{out}}[\mathcal{H}_t \oplus E_{ft}] \\
W_{t,k} &= \text{Sample}_k(\text{Softmax}(\mathcal{W}_{\text{k}}\mathcal{H}_{\text{o}})), \text{k} = 1, \ldots, \text{K}
\end{aligned}
\tag{2}
$$

**Attention with Hierarchical Relative Positional Encoding.** As illustrated in Fig. 1, hierarchical relative positional encoding (HRPE) consists of two key components: bar-level relative positional encoding (Bar-RPE) and section-level relative positional encoding (Section-RPE). The process can be expressed as follows:

$$
\begin{aligned}
Q, K, V &= W_Q X, W_K X, W_V X \\
H_{\text{att}} &= \text{Softmax}(\frac{QK^T + QE_{\text{brpe}} + QE_{\text{srpe}}}{\sqrt{D_h}})V
\end{aligned}
\tag{3}
$$

Here, $X$ represents the output of the input module, and $W_Q$, $W_K$, and $W_V$ are trainable parameters. $E_{\text{brpe}}$ and $E_{\text{srpe}}$ denote the embeddings of Bar-RPE and Section-RPE, respectively. The attention matrix is modified by adding the biases from Bar-RPE and Section-RPE. The resulting tensor is normalized using the softmax function and multiplied with the value matrix $V$ to obtain $H_{\text{att}}$. This modification enables the model to effectively capture the hierarchical structure of the music, leading to improved performance.

### 3.2   Bar-Level Relative Positional Encoding

The concept of Bar-RPE was first introduced in [2], where they employed this method to address the problem of unknown number of tokens during the inference of music score infilling task. However, we show that this design can be used to improve the model performance and contribute to the local structures of generated music pieces. We assume that Bar-RPE is more musically meaningful as Bar-level dependencies have been verified statistically by other researchers [20]. The major difference between Bar-RPE and the common Token-RPE is how the distance of different notes is measured. Instead of using the number of intermediate notes to represent the relative distance between two notes, Bar-RPE adopts the number of intermediate bars as a relative measure. As illustrated in Fig. 2, notes within the same bar share the same Bar-RPE. We use $\mathcal{M}_{\text{brpe}}$ to denote the matrix of relative positions at bar-level, and $E_{\text{brpe}}$ to denote the result of Bar-RPE: $E_{\text{brpe}} = \text{Embedding}_{\text{b}}(\mathcal{M}_{\text{brpe}})$.

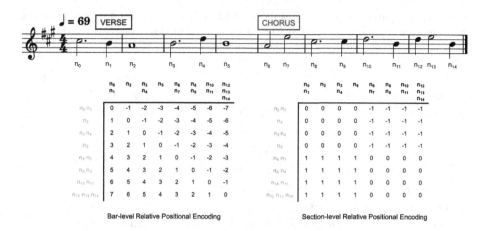

**Fig. 2.** An illustration of Bar-RPE (left) and Section-RPE (right). Each row in the matrix shows the relative position of all tokens within a bar.

### 3.3 Section-Level Relative Positional Encoding

Section-RPE is motivated by the observation that sections of the same type in many popular songs exhibit high correlation, with the chorus section being a typical example of repeated sections with slight variations to shape the listeners' perception of music. While Bar-RPE counts the number of relative bars, Section-RPE is more intricate due to the presence of different types of sections, such as verses and choruses, which can occur multiple times within a song, e.g., $verse_1$-$chorus_1$-$verse_2$-$chorus_2$. The calculation of Section-RPE is based on the switch between these sections. We denote this setting as $S_{a_i} S_{b_j}$, where $a$ and $b$ represent the section types, $i$ and $j$ represent the index of certain section types, e.g., $S_{verse_1} S_{chorus_2}$ denotes the section distance between $verse_1$ and $chorus_2$. The relative distance matrix $\mathcal{M}_{\mathrm{srpe}}$ of Section-RPE, which is illustrated in Fig. 2, represents structural information in a longer context than Bar-RPE. In brief, Section-RPE is formulated to capture the correlation between different sections of the same type and their variations. We use $E_{\mathrm{srpe}}$ to represent the result of Section-RPE: $E_{\mathrm{srpe}} = \mathrm{Embedding}_{\mathrm{s}}(\mathcal{M}_{\mathrm{srpe}})$.

## 4 Implementation Details

### 4.1 Datasets

The scarcity of high-quality annotated data has been a limiting factor for the development of symbolic music generation models. Although some efforts have been made to annotate public datasets with Music Information Retrieval (MIR) techniques [4], the quality of these annotations is often unsatisfactory due to the complexity of defining music semantics. Inaccurate annotations can lead to erroneous conclusions, thus manual annotation of sections was performed on

**Table 1.** Comparison with previous works. NLL refers to Negative Log Likelihood on the validation set and Ep stands for the number of training rounds reaching the lowest NLL. For all the objective metrics, the mean values are reported.

| Group | Datasets | Single-Track NLL@Ep | Multi-Track NLL@Ep |
|---|---|---|---|
| Music Trans. [13] | POP909-S | 0.3392 @ 38 | 0.5005 @ 41 |
| Segatron [1] | POP909-S | 0.2233 @ **28** | 0.4628 @ 45 |
| CPW Trans. [12] | POP909-S | 0.4202 @ 64 | 0.6459 @ 78 |
| Ours | POP909-S | **0.2002** @ 30 | **0.4174 @ 41** |
| Music Trans. [13] | POP2000-S | 0.2630 @ 34 | 0.2504 @ 50 |
| Segatron [1] | POP2000-S | 0.2391 @ **30** | 0.2470 @ 48 |
| CPW Trans. [12] | POP2000-S | 0.3227 @ 53 | 0.3893 @ 98 |
| Ours | POP2000-S | **0.2284** @ 32 | **0.2379 @ 46** |

**Table 2.** Ablation studies of HRPE using Transformer architecture. S-track and M-track respectively represent single-track and multi-track. S-track and M-track respectively represent single track and multi-track.

| NO. | Group | Datasets | S-Track NLL@Ep | M-Track NLL@Ep |
|---|---|---|---|---|
| #1 | HRPE | POP909-S | **0.2002** @ 30 | **0.4174 @ 41** |
| #2 | - Bar-RPE | POP909-S | 0.2014 @ 40 | 0.4238 @ 49 |
| #3 | - Section-RPE | POP909-S | 0.2030 @ 32 | 0.4184 @ 41 |
| #4 | - Bar-RPE - Section-RPE | POP909-S | 0.2083 @ 46 | 0.4346 @ 56 |
| #5 | #4 + Token-RPE | POP909-S | 0.2309 @ **23** | 0.4284 @ 52 |
| #6 | #4 + APE | POP909-S | 0.2449 @ 58 | 0.4544 @ 62 |
| #7 | HRPE | POP2000-S | **0.2284** @ 32 | 0.2379 @ 46 |
| #8 | - Bar-RPE | POP2000-S | 0.2294 @ 42 | 0.2389 @ 56 |
| #9 | - Section-RPE | POP2000-S | 0.2300 @ 35 | **0.2374** @ 42 |
| #10 | - Bar-RPE - Section-RPE | POP2000-S | 0.2376 @ 48 | 0.2472 @ 59 |
| #11 | #10 + Token-RPE | POP2000-S | 0.2488 @ **23** | 0.2503 @ **35** |
| #12 | #10 + APE | POP2000-S | 0.2443 @ 51 | 0.2438 @ 59 |

both the public POP909 [19] dataset and an internal dataset of 2000 multi-track pop songs selected and verified by musicians. These datasets, referred to as POP909-S and POP2000-S, respectively, were used for our experiments. Specifically, the labeled section tags include [Intro], [Verse], [Pre Chorus], [Chorus], [Break], [Bridge], [Outro], and the start and end time of these sections. To the best of our knowledge, our dataset is the first manually annotated dataset of section information in the field of symbolic music and may serve as a foundation for further research. In our experiments, we selected 4/4 beat melodies from both datasets and randomly split them into training and validation sets with a ratio of 95/5 (Table 2).

**Table 3.** Ablation studies of Section-RPE implementation methods based on POP2000-S dataset, where $S_a$ represents the relative position that distinguishes different section types and $S_{a_i}$ represents the relative position that distinguishes both different section types and the number of section occurrences.

| No. | Section-RPE Mode | S-Track NLL—Pitch NLL | M-Track NLL — Pitch NLL |
|-----|------------------|----------------------|------------------------|
| #1 | Baseline | 0.2443 — 0.2985 | 0.2438 — 0.2710 |
| #2 | Conventional RPE | 0.2382 — 0.3000 | 0.2436 — 0.2651 |
| #3 | $S_a S_b$ | 0.2297 — 0.2899 | 0.2392 — 0.2595 |
| #4 | $S_{a_i} S_{b_j}$ | **0.2294 — 0.2884** | **0.2389 — 0.2575** |

## 4.2 Training and Inference Details

The proposed model consists of a 12-layer Transformer decoder with key hyperparameters, such as a learning rate of 1e-4, hidden size of 512, number of attention heads of 8, and FFN hidden size of 2048. Similar to [18], Adam optimizer with default parameters was used for optimization. Notably, the sequence lengths of the single-track and multi-track experiments differ, with the maximum sequence length set to 2048 for single-track experiments and 4096 for multi-track experiments. To overcome the issue of limited training data, data augmentation was performed by randomly adding -6 to +6 to the values of all pitches, as proposed in [13]. This technique effectively reduced the validation loss.

During inference, a combination of temperature sampling and top-p sampling [11] was utilized as the sampling strategy. In particular, temperature sampling was not applied to [pitch] and [type], whereas temperature was set to 1.1 and p to 0.9 for all other predicted elements.

## 5    Experiments and Results

Experiments were conducted on POP909-S and POP2000-S datasets using a Tesla V100 GPU. The training time for single-track tasks was 2 h and 7 h for the former and latter datasets, respectively. For multi-track tasks, the training time increased by a factor of three. To ensure a fair comparison, the same data representation, parameter settings, dictionaries, and data augmentation were used in all experiments. The results were averaged over 10 runs for each experiment.

### 5.1    Quantitative Analysis

**Comparison with Previous Works.** Table 1 presents the results of the objective evaluation. The proposed model achieved better validation NLL results in both single-track and multi-track experiments, indicating its superior performance. Moreover, the convergence speed was also improved compared with music transformer. It is noteworthy that Segatron [1] used a hierarchical positional encoding of token, sentence, and paragraph of text by adding with the input

**Table 4.** The results of the human evaluation on the four evaluation metrics(O: Overall, S: Structure, H: Harmony, D: Diversity), we tested the single-track and multi-track models on the POP909-S and POP2000-S datasets.

| Setting | O | S | H | D | O | S | H | D |
|---|---|---|---|---|---|---|---|---|
| | Single-Track POP909-S | | | | Single-Track POP2000-S | | | |
| Music Trans. [13] | 1.35 | 1.41 | 1.34 | 2.14 | 1.55 | 1.49 | 1.69 | 1.56 |
| CPW Trans. [12] | 1.83 | 1.65 | 1.96 | 2.19 | 1.93 | 1.73 | 1.95 | 1.81 |
| Segatron [1] | 2.27 | 2.04 | 2.69 | 1.89 | 1.62 | 1.57 | 1.69 | 1.49 |
| Ours | **2.67** | **2.49** | **2.84** | **2.44** | **2.43** | **2.41** | **2.45** | **2.22** |
| | Multi-Track POP909-S | | | | Multi-Track POP2000-S | | | |
| Music Trans. [13] | 2.35 | 2.21 | 2.41 | 2.29 | 2.15 | 2.06 | 2.22 | 1.87 |
| CPW Trans. [12] | 2.57 | 2.45 | 2.50 | 2.42 | 1.93 | 1.91 | 2.11 | 1.85 |
| Segatron [1] | 1.50 | 1.27 | 1.75 | 1.92 | 1.31 | 1.29 | 1.49 | 1.38 |
| Ours | **2.79** | **2.65** | **2.94** | **2.63** | **2.55** | **2.58** | **2.46** | **2.33** |

**Table 5.** Pairwise comparisons of subjective evaluation results. The p-values indicate that our proposed model achieved statistically significant improvements ($p < 0.05$).

| Setting | $P_O$ | $P_S$ | $P_H$ | $P_D$ | $P_O$ | $P_S$ | $P_H$ | $P_D$ |
|---|---|---|---|---|---|---|---|---|
| | Single-Track POP909-S | | | | Single-Track POP2000-S | | | |
| Ours VS Music Trans | 0.000 | 0.000 | 0.000 | 0.180 | 0.000 | 0.000 | 0.000 | 0.001 |
| Ours VS CPW Trans | 0.000 | 0.000 | 0.000 | 0.980 | 0.007 | 0.002 | 0.001 | 0.013 |
| Ours VS Segatron | 0.012 | 0.002 | 0.265 | 0.000 | 0.000 | 0.001 | 0.000 | 0.000 |
| | Multi-Track POP909-S | | | | Multi-Track POP2000-S | | | |
| Ours VS Music Trans | 0.001 | 0.009 | 0.000 | 0.000 | 0.041 | 0.051 | 0.185 | 0.010 |
| Ours VS CPW Trans | 0.023 | 0.109 | 0.003 | 0.060 | 0.008 | 0.011 | 0.082 | 0.009 |
| Ours VS Segatron | 0.000 | 0.000 | 0.000 | 0.006 | 0.000 | 0.000 | 0.000 | 0.000 |

word embedding. To demonstrate the effectiveness of our proposed HRPE, a comparison was also made with Segatron's approach, where we treat bar as sentence and section as paragraph.

**Ablation Studies of HRPE.** To demonstrate the effectiveness of each component in HRPE, we conduct ablation studies through the following experiments, as depicted in Table 2: 1) The impact of removing Bar-RPE and Section-RPE is assessed through experiments #1 to #4 and #7 to #10. 2) The influence of Token-RPE is investigated in experiments #5 and #11. 3) The effect of APE is evaluated through experiments #6 and #12.

The experimental findings indicate that: 1) HRPE, which combines Section-RPE and Bar-RPE, yields the best performance in both valid NLL and convergence speed, except for the multi-track experiment on the POP2000-S dataset,

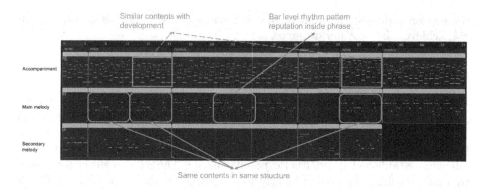

**Fig. 3.** A melody generated by our proposed model.

albeit the difference is negligible. 2) Token-RPE contributes to the model convergence speed in most cases but generally results in higher valid NLL. 3) The addition of APE leads to a significant increase in valid NLL for the POP909-S dataset; however, the increase diminishes as the dataset size expands to 2000. This phenomenon has been investigated in [9, 15].

In order to investigate the contribution of Section-RPE to the quality of generated musical structures, we conducted a comparative analysis of two models utilizing Bar-RPE and HRPE, respectively. Specifically, we generated 50 samples with section tags using each model and enlisted the aid of musicians to manually evaluate the generated structures based on established criteria for popular music. Notably, the model employing HRPE achieved an accuracy rate of 86.7% in terms of structural fidelity, whereas the model utilizing Bar-RPE achieved a comparatively modest accuracy rate of 74.5%. These findings suggest that the use of HRPE may yield improvements in structural accuracy compared to Bar-RPE.

**Ablation Studies of Section-RPE Implementation.** To determine the optimal use of Section-RPE, we analyzed the distribution of distances between identical sections (such as *verse-verse*) in the training dataset. Using sections as distance units, we found that the distance distribution between identical sections was relatively uniform and lacked noticeable regularity. Therefore, we hypothesized that using the conventional RPE calculation method would only provide the model with minimal additional information. To enhance the effectiveness of Section-RPE, we conducted experiments by incorporating information about the type of section and the frequency of its appearance into the calculation of Section-RPE.

From the results presented in Table 3, it can be observed that: 1) Comparing #2 and #1, using the conventional RPE method results in only a slight decrease in valid NLL. 2) Incorporating section type information into Section-RPE, as shown in #3, effectively reduces valid NLL. 3) Combining information about the section type and the number of occurrences of the same section type, as in #4, achieves the best performance.

## 5.2    Human Evaluation

**Comparison with Previous Works.** In the listening test, 20 samples were generated by each model and subsequently mixed in random order. We recruited 15 musicians to evaluate all the samples using a five-point Likert scale based on four perspectives: overall (O), structure (S), harmony (H), and diversity (D), following established standards for popular music. The assessment criteria were rigorous, resulting in predominantly lower scores on the scale. The results of the subjective evaluations for both single-track and multi-track experiments on various datasets are presented in Table 4. Notably, our proposed model outperforms all others in terms of all evaluation metrics across all tasks. The specific p-values of the statistical test are available in the Table 5. Furthermore, compared to previous works, our proposed HRPE yields significant improvements in the structure of both single-track and multi-track samples, suggesting that HRPE is an effective means of enhancing the structural quality of generated music.

**Accuracy of Generated Section Tags.** To assess the accuracy of predicted section tags in relation to the generated music, we enlisted the participation of 10 musicians to evaluate 50 generated samples without any manual selection or modification. The accuracy of the section tags was evaluated based on established criteria for popular music. Following evaluation, we found that the accuracy rate for single-track melodies was 86.7%, while the accuracy rate for multi-track samples was 95.0%. Notably, significant texture changes were observed at various structural transition points. In addition, throughout our experiments, we observed that the baseline model frequently suffered from the degeneration phenomenon, wherein the model fell into endless repetitive loops during inference [11]. We found that HRPE might help mitigate this issue. Specifically, we generated 300 melodies using both the baseline model and our proposed model, with a statistical degradation probability of 32% for the baseline model and only 15% for our proposed model. Similar results were obtained for multi-track tasks.

## 5.3    Case Study

Figure 3 depicts a multi-track sample generated by our proposed model, which consists of three tracks: the main melody, the secondary melody, and the accompaniment. Notably, the section tags corresponding to the melody fragments are also included. Upon analysis of the generated melody, several observations can be made. Firstly, the melody structure conforms to established standards for popular songs, specifically *intro-verse-chorus-break-verse-chorus*, with section tags accurately corresponding to the melody fragments. Secondly, at the section level, similar melodies are observed for the same structures, while significant differences can be observed between different structures. Clear melody changes are also apparent at the transition points between sections. Thirdly, at the bar level, noticeable repetitions and reasonable developments between different bars are observed. These findings demonstrate the ability of our model to generate music that adheres to the hierarchical structure of popular songs, with associations between sections, as well as repetitions and developments between bars.

## 6  Conclusion

In summary, this paper introduces HRPE, a new positional encoding technique that incorporates hierarchical structure information into Transformer. Our proposed approach is demonstrated to be advantageous in both objective and subjective evaluations, exhibiting the ability to generate high-quality pop music with precise and well-organized structures. However, there are some issues to consider, such as the model's reliance on supervised data which necessitates a certain degree of manual annotation. Moving forward, we intend to extend our methods to other music genres and explore their combination with diverse music representations. Additionally, we aim to investigate joint training with unsupervised data.

## References

1. Bai, H., et al.: Segatron: segment-aware transformer for language modeling and understanding. In: Proceedings of the AAAI Conference on Artificial Intelligence, vol. 35, pp. 12526–12534 (2021)
2. Chang, C.J., Lee, C.Y., Yang, Y.H.: Variable-length music score infilling via XLN-ET and musically specialized positional encoding. arXiv preprint arXiv:2108.05064 (2021)
3. Dai, S., Jin, Z., Gomes, C., Dannenberg, R.B.: Controllable deep melody generation via hierarchical music structure representation. Cornell University. arXiv:2109.00663 (2021)
4. Dai, S., Zhang, H., Dannenberg, R.B.: Automatic analysis and influence of hierarchical structure on melody, rhythm and harmony in popular music. Cornell University. arXiv:2010.07518 (2020)
5. Dai, Z., Yang, Z., Yang, Y., Carbonell, J., Le, Q.V., Salakhutdinov, R.: Transformer-xl: attentive language models beyond a fixed-length context. arXiv preprint arXiv:1901.02860 (2019)
6. Dong, H.W., Chen, K., Dubnov, S., McAuley, J., Berg-Kirkpatrick, T.: Multitrack music transformer: learning long-term dependencies in music with diverse instruments. arXiv preprint arXiv:2207.06983 (2022)
7. Dufter, P., Schmitt, M., Schütze, H.: Position information in transformers: an overview. Comput. Linguist. 48(3), 733–763 (2022)
8. Guo, Z., Kang, J., Herremans, D.: A domain-knowledge-inspired music embedding space and a novel attention mechanism for symbolic music modeling. arXiv preprint arXiv:2212.00973 (2022)

9. Haviv, A., Ram, O., Press, O., Izsak, P., Levy, O.: Transformer language models without positional encodings still learn positional information. arXiv preprint arXiv:2203.16634 (2022)
10. He, P., Liu, X., Gao, J., Chen, W.: DeBERTa: decoding-enhanced BERT with disentangled attention. arXiv preprint arXiv:2006.03654 (2020)
11. Holtzman, A., Buys, J., Du, L., Forbes, M., Choi, Y.: The curious case of neural text degeneration. arXiv preprint arXiv:1904.09751 (2019)
12. Hsiao, W.Y., Liu, J.Y., Yeh, Y.C., Yang, Y.H.: Compound word transformer: learning to compose full-song music over dynamic directed hypergraphs. In: Proceedings of the AAAI Conference on Artificial Intelligence, vol. 35, pp. 178–186 (2021)
13. Huang, C.Z.A., et al.: Music transformer: generating music with long-term structure. In: International Conference on Learning Representations (2019)
14. Huang, Y.S., Yang, Y.H.: Pop music transformer: beat-based modeling and generation of expressive pop piano compositions. In: Proceedings of the 28th ACM International Conference on Multimedia, pp. 1180–1188 (2020)
15. Ke, G., He, D., Liu, T.Y.: Rethinking positional encoding in language pre-training. arXiv preprint arXiv:2006.15595 (2020)
16. Lu, P., Tan, X., Yu, B., Qin, T., Zhao, S., Liu, T.Y.: Meloform: generating melody with musical form based on expert systems and neural networks. arXiv preprint arXiv:2208.14345 (2022)
17. Raffel, C., et al.: Exploring the limits of transfer learning with a unified text-to-text transformer. J. Mach. Learn. Res. 21(1), 5485–5551 (2020)
18. Vaswani, A.,et al., Polosukhin, I.: Attention is all you need. In: Advances in Neural Information Processing Systems, vol. 30 (2017)
19. Wang, Z., et al.: Pop909: a pop-song dataset for music arrangement generation. In: International Symposium/Conference on Music Information Retrieval (2020)
20. Yu, B., et al.: Museformer: transformer with fine-and coarse-grained attention for music generation. arXiv preprint arXiv:2210.10349 (2022)
21. Zhang, K., et al.: WuYun: exploring hierarchical skeleton-guided melody generation using knowledge-enhanced deep learning. arXiv preprint arXiv:2301.04488 (2023)
22. Zhang, N.: Learning adversarial transformer for symbolic music generation. IEEE Trans. Neural Networks Learn. Syst. 34, 1754–1763 (2020)
23. Zhang, X., Zhang, J., Qiu, Y., Wang, L., Zhou, J.: Structure-enhanced pop music generation via harmony-aware learning. Cornell University. arXiv:2109.06441 (2021)
24. Zhao, J., Xia, G.: Accomontage: accompaniment arrangement via phrase selection and style transfer. arXiv preprint arXiv:2108.11213 (2021)
25. Zou, Y., Zou, P., Zhao, Y., Zhang, K., Zhang, R., Wang, X.: Melons: generating melody with long-term structure using transformers and structure graph. In: ICASSP 2022–2022 IEEE International Conference on Acoustics, Speech and Signal Processing (ICASSP), pp. 191–195. IEEE (2022)

# Chinese Chorales Dataset: A High-Quality Music Dataset for Score Generation

Yongjie Peng[1], Lei Zhang[2], and Zhenyu Wang[1(✉)]

[1] The School of Control and Computer Engineering, North China Electric Power University, Beijing, China
{yjpeng,zywang}@ncepu.edu.cn
[2] Beijing National Day School-Longyue Experimental Middle School, Beijing, China

**Abstract.** For a long time, the JSB Chorales Dataset has served as the benchmark for choral composition generation, with numerous models and algorithms achieving remarkable results on this dataset, which is designed to generate Bach-style choral music. However, when we aim to tackle the task of generating Chinese vocal choral compositions, we encounter a lack of suitable Chinese music datasets for this purpose. The Chinese Chorales Dataset presented in this paper is a high-quality collection of Chinese choral music, comprising 125 Chinese choral songs stored in MusicXML format, divided into 441 musical segments. This dataset has been professionally crafted to meet the needs of Chinese composers seeking to create high-quality choral compositions. We also provide a compressed .npz file version containing pitch, fermata, tempo, and chord information, split into training, validation, and test sets. Additionally, we conducted multiple experiments on this dataset to validate the effectiveness of the information contained within. For access to the dataset and usage details, please visit https://github.com/123654ad/Chinese-Chorales-Dataset/tree/main.

**Keywords:** music dataset · Chinese chorales · machine learning · benchmark

## 1 Introduction

Musical score is a way of recording music in symbols. It typically deals with symbolic representations and encodes abstract musical features including beats, chords, pitches, durations, and rich structural information. The relationship between musical score and audio is like that between text and speech; a musical score is a highly symbolic and abstract visual representation that effectively records and communicates musical ideas, while audio contains all the details that we can hear. The symbolic generation of musical scores, i.e., Score Generation, is one of the important subtasks of music generation. [4,10]

There are many compositional tasks included in Score Generation, such as: generating a harmonic accompaniment to a given melody, composing a melody based on chords, melody generation, etc. [5,7,8]. Some of these score-generation tasks are automated without constraints, and some are conditionally constrained. Still, most of them are aimed at assisting composers to create more novel and creative songs more easily. In order to accomplish these musical score-generation tasks, a high-quality musical score dataset is essential.

In recent years, the JSB Chorales Dataset [1] and the JSB fake Chorales Dataset is often used for melodic harmony tasks. The goal of this task is to generate a harmonic accompaniment to a given melody. Harmony is one of the basic expressive tools of music, which can add richness and expressiveness to music, and the difficulty of this task lies in ensuring the correct relationship between the generated melody and the harmony. In both datasets, each musical score contains four voices, namely soprano, alto, tenor, and bass, and the soprano voice is usually used as the main melody to generate the other three voices, thus obtaining a vocal chorus in the Bach style.

For the Bach-style dataset, many excellent models have been developed in recent years, such as Choir Transformer [20], DeepChoir [19], BachBot [11], Deep-Bach [6], and so on. These models all utilize deep learning techniques to learn the styles and rules of Bach chorales and are able to generate high-quality and varied choral excerpts.

However, there is a shortage of datasets specifically dedicated to authentic Chinese folk music, especially in polyphonic formats. Additionally, there is a lack of datasets for generating choral compositions featuring human voices singing Chinese folk songs.

Creating such a dataset holds significant value, as it:

Preserves Cultural Heritage: By curating an extensive collection of authentic Chinese folk music in a structured dataset, we effectively preserve and document our rich musical heritage.

Fosters Cultural Expression: Music is a profound expression of cultural identity. This dataset enables composers to infuse their works with the unique character of our cultural traditions. It contributes to the celebration and continued relevance of our cultural identity.

Empowers Creative Exploration: Composers gain access to a valuable resource for inspiration and exploration. They can draw from the extensive pool of Chinese folk melodies, making it easier to incorporate these elements into their compositions. This empowers contemporary composers to create music that echoes our cultural history.

In this paper, we introduce the Chinese Chorales Dataset, a high-quality dataset of Chinese chorales containing 125 choral songs from modern China, all the musical scores were produced by manual scoring, and were segmented into a total of 441 musical score fragments. The dataset is stored in two ways, one in MusicXML format, and the other is a .npz compressed file version containing pitch, fermata, beat, and chord information, which is divided into a training set, a validation set, and a test set.

We hope that our dataset can help in future choral song generation, especially in the following two tasks:

**Table 1.** Existing Datasets for score generation

| Datasets | Dataset information | | | | |
|---|---|---|---|---|---|
| | Size | Polyphony | Choral Music | Annotation | Music Type (Chinese/Western) |
| JSB Chorales Dataset [1] | 380+ | ✓ | ✓ | ✗ | Western |
| JS Fake Chorales Dataset [14] | 500 | ✓ | ✓ | ✗ | Western |
| POP909 [18] | 909 | ✓ | ✗ | ✓ | Chinese-Western mixture |
| Opencpop [17] | 100 | ✗ | ✗ | ✓ | Chinese |
| Lakh MIDI [15] | 170k | ✓ | ✗ | ✗ | Chinese-Western mixture |
| **Chinese Chorales Dataset** | **441** | ✓ | ✓ | ✓ | **Chinese** |

**Task 1**: Generate a complete Chinese vocal chorus based on a given soprano melody, to help Chinese composers create better quality chorus more easily.

**Task 2**: Help composers complete the task of melody generation, generate a whole melody with Chinese national style, and then create a complete song.

This paper has three main contributions:

1. We introduce the Chinese Chorales Dataset, a MusicXML-formatted dataset of Chinese chorales containing a total of 125 chorales divided into 441 musical score segments for storage.
2. We have done several experiments on the Chinese Chorales Dataset to demonstrate the validity of pitch, fermata, beat, and chord information in this dataset.
3. We have curated a Chinese choral music dataset manually transcribed, which addresses the current absence of a readily available Chinese folk song dataset suitable for generating vocal choral compositions. This dataset will facilitate easier creation of Chinese folk songs, contribute to the promotion of Chinese culture, and make Chinese music more accessible to musicians and audiences worldwide.

## 2    Related Work

In this section, we will discuss in Sect. 2.1 some existing musical score datasets, their respective characteristics, and whether they are able to fulfill the purpose of generating Chinese chorales that we wish to accomplish. After that, we will discuss in Sect. 2.2 what requirements our dataset should fulfil in order to accomplish Task 1 and Task 2, which we hope to do.

### 2.1    Existing Music Dataset

The currently available datasets for musical score music generation are summarized in Table 1. The first column in Table 1 shows the name of the dataset and the remaining columns indicate some other information about the dataset, such as the size of the dataset, its format, and whether it contains external information.

One of the popular datasets for chorales generation is JSB Chorales, which is available in several versions, with the common version containing a total of 380+ musical score fragments. Each musical score fragment contains four voice parts: soprano, alto, tenor, and bass. JSB fake Chorales [14] provides 500 musical score fragments generated by TonicNet [13]in MIDI format by using models with narrow expertise as a source of high-quality scalable synthesis data.

However, neither dataset provides external labels such as beats, chords, etc., and by providing external labels the controllability of the dataset can be effectively improved [2,16], as well as making it easier to evaluate the performance of the generated models. [9]

POP909 [18] provides a dataset of piano arrangements of multiple versions of 909 popular songs composed by professional musicians, which provides rhythmic, metric, key, and chord annotations for each song. POP909 has now also become one of the well-known datasets for polyphonic music generation, but the 'polyphony' it provides is vocal melody, lead melody, and piano accompaniment, rather than multi-part choral pieces.

Lakh MIDI is one of the most popular datasets in notation format, containing 176,581 songs in MIDI format from a wide range of genres, produced by a PhD at Columbia University [15]. Most of the songs in this dataset have multiple tracks, most of which are consistent with the original audio.

None of the datasets mentioned above are purely Chinese song datasets, and therefore, they do not meet our expectations for the task of creating high-quality Chinese choral songs.

In addition to the above datasets, Opencpop serves as a publicly available high-quality Mandarin singing corpus for singing voice synthesis (SVS). The corpus consists of 100 popular Chinese songs sung by a professional female singer. The audio files are recorded in studio quality at a sampling rate of 44,100 Hz, with corresponding lyrics and musical scores.

Although Opencpop is a pure Chinese pop song dataset, it is not a choral song dataset containing multiple voices.

Hence, in pursuit of our ultimate goal of automating the composition of Chinese chorales, it becomes imperative for us to develop a dedicated chorales dataset comprising exclusively authentic Chinese musical content.

The creation of such a dataset is a fundamental step towards enabling advanced AI and machine learning systems to not only understand the intricacies of traditional Chinese musical composition but also to foster innovation in this realm. By exclusively focusing on Chinese music, we can preserve the essence of Chinese musical heritage and pave the way for the automated generation of new Chinese chorales that respect and perpetuate these deep-rooted traditions.

Moreover, this specialized dataset serves as a crucial bridge between technology and culture, facilitating the seamless integration of traditional Chinese musical elements into contemporary music. It is a testament to the harmonious coexistence of technology and cultural heritage, empowering the next generation of musicians and composers to create and share music that is rich in Chinese cultural identity on both local and global stages.

From Table 1, our dataset is comparable in terms of data volume to other existing datasets such as Opencpop, JSB Chorales Dataset, and JS Fake Chorales Dataset. However, our dataset stands out as it encompasses "polyphonic" vocal Chinese music scores and includes external annotations. These characteristics, unique to our dataset, enable it to undertake tasks that other datasets cannot accomplish, such as **Task 1**.

### 2.2    Requirements for the Choral Music Dataset

To fulfill our expectation of realizing a dataset of Chinese choral songs, we first identified the requirements that need to be met for the production of this dataset [12,16], The requirements are as follows.:

**Four Voices:** to provide valid information for the generation of chorales in Task 1.

**Chinese Music:** to meet our expectation of creating Chinese chorales.

**External Annotation:** to ensure the controllability of the generation process and the evaluability of the generation results. [2,16]

## 3    Dataset Description and External Annotation Methods

Chinese Chorales Dataset is a musical score dataset consisting entirely of Chinese chorales, providing choral musical scores for a total of 125 songs. In the following Sect. 3.1, we will talk about the production process of the dataset in detail, and in Sect. 3.2, we will describe the format of the dataset and the external annotations we give.

### 3.1    Dataset Production Process

In order to collect a dataset of Chinese songs with contemporary features and ethnic flavors, we have hired professional composers to re-arrange Chinese songs obtained from the Internet into four-part musical scores. These songs are primarily from the last century to the present and revolve around patriotic themes. We will release the list of the song titles list along with the dataset.

We followed the following process to collect and process the dataset:

1. Initially, we selected songs that met our criteria based on their time period and style, ensuring that these songs exhibited relatively consistent historical characteristics and musical styles. We conducted searches on the internet to find and download the sheet music for these songs.
2. After the preliminary selection of musical compositions, we engaged professional composers to re-arrange the chosen songs, creating four-part musical scores in MusicXML format. These scores were stored on local servers and backed up in the cloud.

**Table 2.** Examples of chord information

| Chord | Interval | Root | Duration |
|-------|----------|------|----------|
| Song1 | $[0,3,7]$ $[0,3,7]$ | C4 C4 | 1 1 |

**Table 3.** Examples of pitch information

| Pitch | Soprano, Alto, Tenor, Bass |
|-------|----------------------------|
| Song1 | $[63, 58, 70, 67]$<br>$[63, 58, 72, 67]$<br>$[63, 58, 70, 67]$ |
| Song2 | $[76, 67, 71, 0]$<br>$[76, 67, 74, 0]$<br>... |

3. Furthermore, we assigned a group of individuals to review the composed musical scores. They meticulously assessed and compared each song to ensure that they retained the essence and unique characteristics of the original songs. They also coordinated the styles of various choral pieces, ensuring that all songs in the dataset met our requirements and goals.

### 3.2 Dataset Format

We saved our dataset in the MusicXML data format, and we used the Music21 library for the processing and saving of datasets in the MusicXML format. [3]

In addition to the musical score fragments saved in MusicXML format, we also provide .npz compressed files containing pitch information, fermata, beat information, and chord information. Each of these files is a dictionary containing the training set, validation set, and test set, where the corresponding value for each song is a list of sequences.

The example pitch sequences are given in Table 2, from which we can get a rough idea of how the pitch sequences are stored in the Chinese Chorales Dataset.

The number of musical score segments contained in the training, validation, and test sets are 309, 88, and 44, respectively. In a file containing pitch information, each sequence is itself a list of time steps, and at each time step, there are four numbers corresponding to one pitch for each voice.

The pitches are encoded as 0–129, which contains 128 pitches, a rest, and a hold, with the time resolution set to 16th notes. In the file containing the fermata information, the fermata is represented by 0, 1, and the beat is encoded as 0–3, which represents no beat, weak beat, medium-heavy beat, and strong beat, respectively. [19]

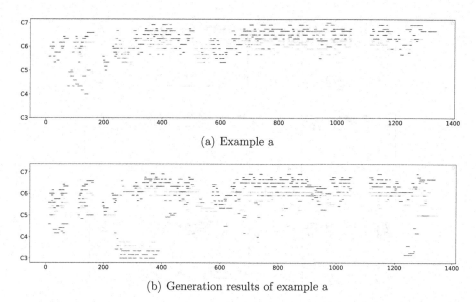

(a) Example a

(b) Generation results of example a

**Fig. 1.** Example generated using the Chinese chorus dataset. In this example, the green part is the main melody, the orange part is the alto, the blue part is the tenor, and the red part is the bass.The generative model uses Deepchoir (full) with sixteenth note resolution. (Color figure online)

As for the information in the chord section, the previous practice tends to encode some chords that are commonly used; the authors of TonicNet encoded chords into fifty categories, namely twelve major chords (one chord for each pitch category in the Western chromatic scale), twelve minor chords, twelve diminished chords, twelve augmented chords and special notation [13], while the authors of DeepChoir coded into twelve categories. [19]

Considering the large number of chord categories contained in this dataset, and to represent the various categories as completely as possible, so that the users of this dataset can encode the chord categories by themselves according to their own needs, this paper adopts the representation of intervals, roots and durations. The duration is expressed in quarter notes, and a duration of 1 means that the chord lasts one-quarter note.

As shown in Table 3, this approach not only provides a complete representation of each chord but also adds the durations of different chords to the model, which provides more complete and rich information. The four columns in Table 3 show the corresponding song, the chord's interval, the chord's duration, and the chord's root note (the lowest note).

(a) Original Musical score Fragment.

(b) Musical score fragment generated with DeepChoir(full)

**Fig. 2.** Comparison of the musical score fragment generated using DeepChoir(full) with the original fragment

## 4    Experiments

In this section, we conduct a baseline experiment on music generation using the Chinese Chorales Dataset: choral song generation conditional on melody. We conducted the experiment using several models, including DeepChoir [19], BachBot [11], and DeepBach [6]. These three models have shown very good results on the JSB Chorales Dataset and are also well-known models under this task. Therefore, we decided to test our dataset on these models.

### 4.1    Model and Parameter Settings

To ensure that the various information in our dataset is reliable, we modified the publicly available code in [19] and conducted several experiments.

We first cut the two-channel structure in the DeepChoir model, leaving only the branch used to input pitch information. We tested the learnability of the pitch information of the dataset by inputting only pitch information to the model in this way, and the experiments ultimately determined that the model was able

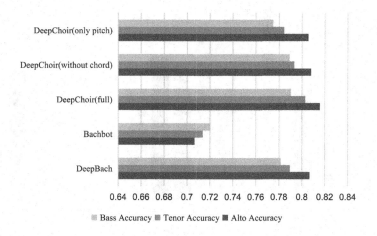

**Fig. 3.** Comparison of the generation accuracy of each model for the three voices

to learn valid information from the pitch information alone, thus generating chorales with a high degree of accuracy that could be convincing.

Secondly, we tried the effect of adding beat and intensity information to pitch information, and chord information, respectively. It is worth mentioning that during these multiple experiments, we removed the gamma sampling algorithm from our code, as it was found that post-processing methods such as the gamma sampling algorithm mentioned in [8] would have a large impact on the generation of our dataset.

In contrast, we did not make any changes in the DeepBach and Bach-Bot models. All the experiments we conducted were trained with the same parameters.

## 4.2   Results

Figure 1 shows an example of DeepChoir(full) generation, where the top piano roll is a fragment of the score from the dataset, and the bottom piano roll is the generated score, with the main theme in green, alto in orange, tenor in blue, and bass in red.

The musical score fragment generated with DeepChoir(full) is shown in Fig. 2 along with the original musical score fragment. As can be seen in Fig. 1 and 2, the generated scores capture the basic harmonic relationship between melody and accompaniment and contain consistent rhythmic patterns. While the quality leaves something to be desired, it serves as a baseline to illustrate the usage of our dataset.

Figure 3 shows the generation results of the above three models, and it can be seen that all three models can achieve a high correct rate on the Chinese Chorales Dataset. Meanwhile, on the DeepChoir model, the order of the correct rates of the three voices is also in line with our expectation, i.e., the model containing only pitch information has the lowest correct rate, the one with fermata information

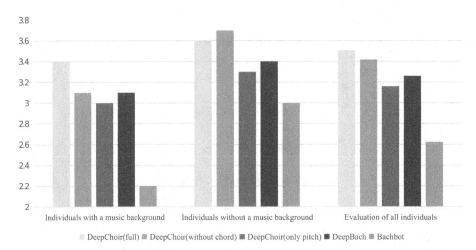

**Fig. 4.** Subjective evaluation scores of each model

and beat information has a slightly higher correct rate, and the one with chord information has an even higher rate.

In addition to objective evaluation criteria, we also conducted subjective assessments. We invited 34 students to provide feedback on our generated results, with 16 of them possessing a certain level of music background, while the remaining 18 students evaluated the results without any prior musical knowledge. All evaluators assigned scores to the musical scores on a scale of 1–5 based on the perceived quality of the songs.

As shown in Fig. 4, although the evaluations from individuals without a music background deviated slightly from our expectations, the final evaluation results were generally consistent with our expectations. Specifically, the Deepchoir (full) model, which incorporates all four types of information as input, produced the best results. This demonstrates that when all four specified types of information are provided as input, the model can more effectively learn the compositional patterns from the main melody to the various vocal parts, resulting in the creation of chorale compositions that are generally well-received by the audience.

Through the analysis of multiple experiments employing both subjective and objective evaluation criteria, we conclude that the four pieces of information in our dataset are effective and valuable for assisting the model in learning the patterns of choral composition.

## 5   Conclusion

In this paper, we have produced the Chinese Chorales Dataset, a dataset of Chinese chorales. It contains 125 Chinese chorales, which are divided into 441 parts and stored in MusicXML format. We also provide a compressed file version containing pitch, fermata, beat, and chord information. In order to ensure the quality of the data, we used manual scoring to create the dataset, and we designed several experiments on the dataset to verify the validity of the information in the dataset. We hope that this dataset can help in the future task of composing Chinese choral music.

# References

1. Boulanger-Lewandowski, N., Bengio, Y., Vincent, P.: Modeling temporal dependencies in high-dimensional sequences: application to polyphonic music generation and transcription. arXiv preprint arXiv:1206.6392 (2012)
2. Chen, K., Zhang, W., Dubnov, S., Xia, G., Li, W.: The effect of explicit structure encoding of deep neural networks for symbolic music generation. In: 2019 International Workshop on Multilayer Music Representation and Processing (MMRP), pp. 77–84. IEEE (2019)
3. Cuthbert, M.S., Ariza, C.T.: music21: a toolkit for computer-aided musicology and symbolic music data. In: Proceedings of the 11th International Society for Music Information Retrieval Conference, ISMIR 2010, Utrecht, Netherlands, 9–13 August 2010. DBLP (2010)
4. Elowsson, A., Friberg, A.: Algorithmic composition of popular music. In: The 12th International Conference on Music Perception and Cognition and The 8th Triennial Conference of the European Society for The Cognitive Sciences of Music, pp. 276–285 (2012)
5. Gardner, J., Simon, I., Manilow, E., Hawthorne, C., Engel, J.: Mt3: multi-task multitrack music transcription. arXiv preprint arXiv:2111.03017 (2021)
6. Hadjeres, G., Pachet, F., Nielsen, F.: DeepBach: a steerable model for Bach chorales generation. In: International Conference on Machine Learning, pp. 1362–1371. PMLR (2017)
7. Hernandez-Olivan, C., Beltran, J.R.: Music composition with deep learning: a review. In: Advances in Speech and Music Technology: Computational Aspects and Applications, pp. 25–50 (2022)
8. Hernandez-Olivan, C., Puyuelo, J.A., Beltran, J.R.: Subjective evaluation of deep learning models for symbolic music composition. arXiv preprint arXiv:2203.14641 (2022)
9. Hernandez-Olivan, C., Zay Pinilla, I., Hernandez-Lopez, C., Beltran, J.R.: A comparison of deep learning methods for timbre analysis in polyphonic automatic music transcription. Electronics 10(7), 810 (2021)
10. Ji, S., Luo, J., Yang, X.: A comprehensive survey on deep music generation: multilevel representations, algorithms, evaluations, and future directions. arXiv preprint arXiv:2011.06801 (2020)
11. Liang, F.T., Gotham, M., Johnson, M., Shotton, J.: Automatic stylistic composition of Bach chorales with deep LSTM. In: ISMIR, pp. 449–456 (2017)
12. Manilow, E., Wichern, G., Seetharaman, P., Le Roux, J.: Cutting music source separation some Slakh: a dataset to study the impact of training data quality and quantity. In: 2019 IEEE Workshop on Applications of Signal Processing to Audio and Acoustics (WASPAA), pp. 45–49. IEEE (2019)
13. Peracha, O.: Improving polyphonic music models with feature-rich encoding. arXiv preprint arXiv:1911.11775 (2019)
14. Peracha, O.: JS fake chorales: a synthetic dataset of polyphonic music with human annotation. arXiv preprint arXiv:2107.10388 (2021)

15. Raffel, C.: Learning-based methods for comparing sequences, with applications to audio-to-MIDI alignment and matching. Doctoral dissertation (2016)
16. Su, L.: Attend to chords: improving harmonic analysis of symbolic music using transformer-based models (2021)
17. Wang, Y., et al.: Opencpop: a high-quality open source Chinese popular song corpus for singing voice synthesis. arXiv preprint arXiv:2201.07429 (2022)
18. Wang, Z., et al.: POP909: a pop-song dataset for music arrangement generation. arXiv preprint arXiv:2008.07142 (2020)
19. Wu, S., Li, X., Sun, M.: Chord-conditioned melody harmonization with controllable harmonicity. In: ICASSP 2023–2023 IEEE International Conference on Acoustics, Speech and Signal Processing (ICASSP), pp. 1–5. IEEE (2023)
20. Zhou, J., Zhu, H., Wang, X.: Choir transformer: generating polyphonic music with relative attention on transformer. arXiv preprint arXiv:2308.02531 (2023)

# Author Index

X. Li et al. (Eds.): SOMI 2023, CCIS 2007, p. 147, 2024.
https://doi.org/10.1007/978-981-97-0576-4

Printed in the United States
by Baker & Taylor Publisher Services